S0-BYA-429

Peggy Dymond Leavey

Chris McArthur

Peggy Dymond Leavey was born in Toronto. Because her father was in the RCAF, she spent her early years moving from one Canadian military base to another. The second in a family of five children, Peggy started writing at a young age. Her earliest efforts were poems, plays for her "front porch productions," and stories to entertain her youngest sister.

Peggy has since published numerous magazine and newspaper articles, several short stories for children's publications, and been a contributing editor for three books of local history. Her novels for young readers have been nominated for several awards, including the Silver Birch Award, the Manitoba Young Readers' Choice Award, the Arthur Ellis Award, and the Canadian Library Association Book of the Year for Children Award.

Peggy's tenth book, a YA historical fiction, *Growing Up Ivy*, published by Dundurn in 2010, was a starred selection in the Canadian Children's Book Centre's *Best Books for Kids & Teens 2011*. Her most recent title, *Mary Pickford: Canada's Silent Siren; America's Sweetheart*, a Quest Biography, was published by Dundurn in September 2011.

Peggy retired in 2006 after seventeen years as a public librarian in beautiful Prince Edward County. Today, when she's not writing, she enjoys reading and spending time in the outdoors. Peggy is a member of The Writers' Union of Canada, the Canadian Society of Children's Authors, Illustrators & Performers (CANSCAIP), the Canadian Children's Book Centre, the Arts Council of Northumberland, Spirit of the Hills (Northu and the Quinte Arts Council.

The grandmother of eight, she lives Trenton, Ontario.

971.034092 Secor -L

Leavey, P.
Laura Secord.

PRICE: $19.99 (3559/he)

A QUEST BIOGRAPHY

LAURA SECORD

HEROINE OF THE WAR OF 1812

PEGGY DYMOND LEAVEY

DUNDURN
TORONTO

Copyright © Peggy Dymond Leavey, 2012

All rights reserved. No part of this publication may be reproduced, stored in a retrieval system, or transmitted in any form or by any means, electronic, mechanical, photocopying, recording, or otherwise (except for brief passages for purposes of review) without the prior permission of Dundurn Press. Permission to photocopy should be requested from Access Copyright.

Editor: Allison Hirst
Design: Jennifer Scott
Printer: Transcontinental

Library and Archives Canada Cataloguing in Publication

Leavey, Peggy Dymond
    Laura Secord : heroine of the War of 1812 / Peggy Dymond Leavey.

(A Quest biography)
Includes bibliographical references and index.
Issued also in electronic formats.
ISBN 978-1-4597-0366-7

1. Secord, Laura, 1775-1868. 2. Canada--History--War of 1812. I. Title. II. Series: Quest biography

FC443.S4L43 2012   971.03'4092   C2012-900116-3

1   2   3   4   5   16   15   14   13   12

 Conseil des Arts   Canada Council   Canada    ONTARIO ARTS COUNCIL
du Canada   for the Arts   CONSEIL DES ARTS DE L'ONTARIO

We acknowledge the support of the Canada Council for the Arts and the Ontario Arts Council for our publishing program. We also acknowledge the financial support of the Government of Canada through the Canada Book Fund and Livres Canada Books, and the Government of Ontario through the Ontario Book Publishing Tax Credit and the Ontario Media Development Corporation.

Care has been taken to trace the ownership of copyright material used in this book. The author and the publisher welcome any information enabling them to rectify any references or credits in subsequent editions.

J. Kirk Howard, President

Printed and bound in Canada.
www.dundurn.com

Dundurn
3 Church Street, Suite 500
Toronto, Ontario, Canada
M5E 1M2

Gazelle Book Services Limited
White Cross Mills
High Town, Lancaster, England
LA1 4XS

Dundurn
2250 Military Road
Tonawanda, NY
U.S.A. 14150

For my family,
Everyday heroes

Braver deeds are not recorded,
In historic treasures hoarded
Than the march of Laura Secord
Through the forest, long ago.

— Dr. Jakeway (quoted by S.A. Curzon in
Laura Secord & Other Poems, 1887)

Contents

Acknowledgements

I am most grateful to Michael Carroll, associate publisher and editorial director at Dundurn Press for offering me this project and to Allison Hirst for her skillful editing. Everyone at Dundurn that I've had the pleasure of working with has been not only knowledgeable, but also supportive and eager to help, and I thank them all for that.

While writing this book I visited the Niagara Historical Society and Museum in Niagara-on-the-Lake and was able to see for myself their extensive collection of artifacts, including several personal items that had belonged to Laura Secord. I must also acknowledge the numerous publications of the Niagara Historical Society and Museum that are available online. I continue to be grateful for the system of interlibrary loans that has enabled me to access books on Laura Secord as well as on the War of 1812, which provided the backdrop to a large part of Laura's story.

There are few known details of Laura Ingersoll Secord's earliest years in the United States (1775–95), many of which were spent amidst the turmoil of the American Revolution and the War of Independence. Charles Taylor's book, *History of Great Barrington (Berkshire County), Massachusetts*, published in 1892, helped me to fill in some of the blanks. Another book, *The Housatonic: Puritan River* by Chard Powers Smith, published in 1924, I found useful for visualizing the physical surroundings of Laura's first twenty years.

Prologue

In 1860, when she was already eighty-five, Laura Secord insisted that she be allowed to put her signature, along with those of other veterans of the War of 1812, on an address to be presented to the visiting Prince of Wales at a special ceremony at Queenston Heights.

The following year the prince, the future King Edward VII, sent Laura a gift of £100 in gold. It was a reward for her service to her country and the Crown, an act of courage in June 1813 when she had walked nineteen miles (thirty kilometres) — alone and through dangerous territory — to warn a handful of officers at a British outpost of an impending attack by five hundred American soldiers.

When the press picked up the story of the prince's gift, everyone wanted to know more about the woman who'd been the recipient of the royal generosity. Among those who read the newspaper accounts in 1861 was Niagara resident Emma Currie. She would later become one of Laura Secord's earliest and most respected biographers.

Born Emma Augusta Harvey, Mrs. Currie had spent more than a quarter-century in the little village of St. Davids, near Queenston. There she'd been surrounded by Secords, had listened to numerous stories of the War of 1812, but had never heard any mention of Laura's name. Now curious, she questioned an elderly resident and learned that what the newspapers were reporting about this woman's bravery was true.

When the Women's Literary Club was formed in St. Catharines in 1892, Emma Currie, as its founder, wrote a paper to be delivered at the opening, choosing as her subject Laura Secord. During her research, Currie had been surprised to discover that

Courtesy Library and Archives Canada, C-011053.

Meeting Between Laura Secord and Lieutenant James FitzGibbon, June 1813. Artist Lorne K. Smith.

Laura's ancestors, like her own, had come from Great Barrington, Massachusetts. That paper inevitably grew into a book.

Emma Currie had earlier corresponded with Sarah Anne Curzon, the British-born feminist and the author of poems, a play, and a short biography of Laura Secord. Curzon's play, *Laura Secord, the Heroine of 1812*, generated enough interest in Laura that stories and articles about her began to appear in Canadian history books and school texts.

Currie had hoped to be able to access Curzon's research collection for her book, but Sarah Curzon had died in 1898. Janet Carnochan, a respected local historian and co-founder of the Niagara Historical Society, provided Currie with information about the history of Niagara, and she was most fortunate to be able to interview Laura's great-niece and granddaughter.

Emma Currie's book, *The Story of Laura Secord and Canadian Reminiscences*, was published in 1900. It contains a copy of the only known autograph of Laura Secord, and the portrait in the front is taken from what is believed to be the only authentic portrait of the heroine. Even today, Currie's book remains a respected source of expert information.

If an old lady had not been so determined to be included on the prince's address, and if his gift had gone unnoticed by the press, the public might have continued to be unaware of the heroine who'd lived among them, unheralded, for forty-seven years.

1

Child of the Revolution

Eight-year-old Laura Ingersoll kept her eyes squarely on the middle of her aunt's back as the woman left the house carrying the baby.

"This is best, child," Papa had said when he told Laura, right after her mother's funeral, about the arrangement for Abigail to be adopted by the Nashes. "I know you think you can look after your baby sister, but she's still an infant. Believe me, Laura, this is what your mother wanted."

How could that be? Over the past few days Mama had told her again and again how proud she was of the way her eldest daughter had taken over the care of the baby when she herself got sick. "A real little mother, that's what you are, Laura dear."

Was it only a week ago that Laura had sat beside the big four-poster bed, squeezing cool water from a rag and laying it on her mother's fevered brow? "There, child," Elizabeth had said, her voice a hoarse whisper. "You've done enough." Gently, she took Laura's hand away. "You've rocked Abigail to sleep. Just leave the cloth in the wash dish; I can reach it. Take the little girls out for some air. Please, dear. Papa's home now."

"It's cold this morning." Laura's father spoke from the doorway.

"The girls all have warm scarves and mittens, Thomas." Elizabeth gave a rasping cough. "Bundle them up, Laura dear, and take them out. For a little bit."

Mrs. Daniel Nash made her way down the path to the front gate where the horse and cart were waiting. Papa had gone out first to load Abigail's cradle, and now he stood in the road, talking to Uncle Daniel.

Laura snatched her shawl off the peg. If she hurried she could say one last good-bye to her baby sister, kiss again the rosy lips, and breathe in the baby's sweet, milky scent.

"Run up and check that we haven't forgotten anything, Laura." Papa came striding back, turning her around, steering her inside, and closing the door.

But the corner that had been Abigail's for six short months in her parents' upstairs bedroom was bare, and when Laura came back down, the horse and the cart and its three occupants had left.

On February 28, 1775, in Great Barrington, Berkshire County, in the colony of Massachusetts, Thomas Ingersoll had married Elizabeth (Betsy) Dewey, who was just seventeen. Seven months later, on September 13, 1775, Elizabeth gave birth to the couple's first child, a baby girl they named Laura.

Thomas Ingersoll, the father of the girl who would be Laura Ingersoll Secord, was the fifth generation of his family to live in the colony of Massachusetts. The first Ingersoll to set foot on the shores of North America was Richard, coming from Bedfordshire, England, to Salem, Massachusetts, in 1629.

Thomas was born in Westfield, Massachusetts, in 1749, moving to Great Barrington the year before his marriage to Elizabeth. The town, close to the border of the colony of New York, had been settled in 1724 by one hundred families from Westfield. The family of Laura's young mother had also come from Westfield, and Elizabeth, born January 28, 1758, was the daughter of Israel Dewey.

In 1775, Thomas Ingersoll bought a small piece of land with a house on it that, according to some sources, had been built by a man named Daniel Rathbun. Other sources state that the property had been left to Thomas by his grandfather, and that the building on the land had once been a family cottage that young Thomas had enjoyed visiting while he still lived in Westfield.

Already a successful merchant, Thomas Ingersoll set up business in Great Barrington as a hatter — making, selling, and repairing hats. In 1782 he would buy another strip of land to increase the size of his property, and he built a larger home to house his growing family. The house sat on the crest of five acres that rolled gently down to the Housatonic River.

The Housatonic, meaning "place or river beyond the mountains," had been given its name by the Mohicans, a Native American tribe that came over from the Hudson River Valley to use the area as a summer hunting ground. Later, English settlers harnessed the river to power sawmills, gristmills, and to run the furnaces for the working of iron.

The Housatonic River begins its journey of 149 miles in southwestern Massachusetts. As it flows toward Great Barrington it is narrow and swift, dropping several elevations before emerging from the Berkshire Hills.

The Ingersoll home on the main street of the town was a large house, and it was filled with comfortable furnishings befitting a family of privilege. Photographs show the house shaded by mature trees. There is a porch along the right side with a single window above it. A kitchen and servants' quarters for the elderly couple who had worked for the family for many years were later added to the back of the house, and off to the right sat Thomas's shop.

In April 1775, a few months before Laura's birth, the American Revolution had erupted in Massachusetts, with battles in Lexington, Concord, and Bunker Hill.

At the time, America consisted of thirteen colonies: Massachusetts and Maine being one, New Hampshire, Rhode Island, Connecticut, New York, New Jersey, Pennsylvania, Delaware, Maryland, Virginia, North Carolina, South Carolina, and Georgia. In every colony the conflict divided families, some siding with the "colonial patriots" and others with the British Loyalists. It was impossible to remain neutral.

Thomas Ingersoll had no grudge against his Loyalist neighbours, but because he wanted to protect his property and his business from harsh British laws, he chose to fight on the side of the patriots. Before long his young wife would become used to having him march off to daily arms drills while the drums of war grew louder.

One of Thomas's relatives, David Ingersoll, a magistrate and lawyer in Great Barrington, remained a Loyalist, and like many who sided with the British he was victimized by unruly mobs of patriots who took the law into their own hands. After being forcibly driven from his home, he was seized and taken to prison in Connecticut. His house was vandalized, attacked by both swords and hatchets, and all his property destroyed. Eventually, David Ingersoll fled to England.

Anyone caught helping a Loyalist to escape was himself fined or imprisoned, and citizens were paid to turn in their neighbours. Some Loyalists suffered the cruel humiliation of tarring and feathering or were forced to ride a rail through town, which meant sitting upright astride a narrow rail that was carried on the shoulders of two men.

The records of Great Barrington for the year 1776 list Thomas Ingersoll as the town constable and tax collector. When Great Barrington's militia was consolidated into one company in October 1777, Thomas was commissioned second lieutenant under Captain Silas Goodrich. He became captain of the company in October 1781, after marching forty of his men out in response to an alarm raised at Stillwater, New York, the town where part of the Battle of Saratoga had taken place in June of that year.

During Laura's earliest years, spent amidst the noise and confusion of war, her father was often away from home, and the little girl grew close to her gentle mother. A second child, Elizabeth Franks, was born October 17, 1779, and two years later a third daughter, Mira (also spelled Myra), was born. Daughter number four, Abigail, would arrive on the scene in September 1783.

Britain's national debt had doubled after its victory over France and Spain in the Seven Years' War (1756–1763). Now that those two countries no longer posed a threat to the Americans, Britain felt the grateful colonists should help pay more of the cost of colonial government.

The British parliament passed the *Revenue Act of 1764* to raise customs revenues, and the same year the *Currency Act* prohibited the use of colonial paper money. Revenue collectors were appointed to enforce the tax laws, and trade with foreign countries was restricted.

The *Stamp Act* was passed by British parliament in 1765 to levy internal taxes, and the *Quartering Act* forced Americans to pay for housing British troops. It went on and on.

The colonies opposed these policies that were set by a government three thousand miles away, and the cry went out: "no taxation without representation." American merchants joined forces to boycott British businessmen.

The *Tea Act* of 1773 reduced the tax on imported British tea, giving it an unfair advantage. The act allowed the almost-bankrupt British East India Company to sell its tea directly to colonial agents, bypassing American wholesalers. Now those powerful wholesalers had been handed a burning issue.

The American colonists condemned the *Tea Act* and planned to boycott tea. The end result was the infamous Boston Tea Party. When three British tea ships docked in Boston Harbor, men disguised as Indians boarded the vessels and threw all the tea overboard. Punishment was swift.

The Intolerable Acts of 1774 (so-named by the Americans) temporarily closed the port of Boston until compensation was paid, "royalized" the Massachusetts government, expanded the *Quartering Act*, and changed the *Justice Act* so that Americans charged with crimes had to be tried in England. These actions served to unite the colonies, and a call went out from the Virginia Burgesses to convene a continental congress in Philadelphia in 1774 to discuss their grievances.

Among the factions present at that First Continental Congress were those who believed that in the end force would be necessary; the moderates, who urged a peaceful solution; and those who felt Britain must soften its policies but who opposed the use of force and would never approve of independence.

In Congress, the colonists came close to declaring dominion status. They continued to recognize the Crown as necessary to hold them together, and they petitioned King George III for a remedy to their grievances. On the other hand, they asked the French Canadians to join them in their demands and again adopted an economic boycott of Britain.

The Suffolk Resolves of Massachusetts, declaring the Intolerable Acts void and advising the training of a militia force, received the backing of the colonists. When the British government refused to budge, the Americans knew they must come up with a more active resistance.

The local government in Massachusetts had been dissolved by the British, and yet it continued to operate. To remedy this, British general Thomas Gage set out to seize the colony's government leaders, John Hancock and Samuel Adams, as well as the ammunition that was being stored in Concord, just outside Boston.

On April 18, 1775, British troops advanced on Concord. Before the British soldiers reached Lexington, Adams and Hancock managed to escape, having been alerted by Paul Revere. The British were met by the Massachusetts "minutemen," and the American Revolution began.

In May, the Second Continental Congress adopted the poorly organized but growing New England Army outside Boston and chose as its commander General George Washington. Still uncertain about complete independence, Congress petitioned King George to restore peace.

The June 17, 1775 Battle of Bunker Hill, near Boston, was a British victory won at a terrible cost in lives. Nine months later, when General George Washington fortified the heights above

Boston Harbor with cannons, British general William Howe, the successor to General Thomas Gage, feared a repeat of the carnage. He decided against attack and retreated, withdrawing his ships from Boston Harbor. When the British pulled out, 1,100 Loyalists left with them.

During the long siege of Boston the patriots had come to realize that the only means of safeguarding their liberty was going to be through complete independence from Britain.

Congress adopted the Declaration of Independence on July 4, 1776. Now the patriots had a firm commitment: they were fighting for the freedom of the country. It is estimated that about seventy thousand Loyalists fled to Canada, where the women and children found shelter and the men joined the Loyalist regiments.

The American patriots raised a small army of state regiments — the Continental Army — that could be counted on to provide most of the resistance, and it made use of state militia if and when it was available. In the later years of the war the patriots were joined by thousands of French troops, more than happy to help the Americans against their old enemy. For their part, unable to raise enough men at home, the British hired German troops and counted on additional support from the Indians and Loyalists.

After evacuating Boston, British general William Howe seized New York, most of New Jersey, and was not stopped until he reached Trenton at Christmas 1776. The following summer he retaliated by taking Philadelphia.

In the autumn of 1777, British general John Burgoyne led his army in an overland march from Canada toward New York, where he planned to join up with General Howe. They were cut off and captured at Saratoga, New York, in October 1777 by American general Horatio Gates. Burgoyne's surrender of his army of over five thousand men was a huge victory for the Americans, and because it prevented the British from separating New England from the southern colonies, it was a turning point in the war.

Also surrendering with Burgoyne at Saratoga was Baron Friedrich Adolph Riedesel, commander of a regiment of soldiers from the Duchy of Brunswick, one of the German units hired by the British. Following the surrender, American general Horatio Gates treated Burgoyne as a gentleman, refusing to accept his sword and inviting him to his tent.

The allied army had left Canada feeling confident of an easy victory, and many of the officers' wives had accompanied the men, promising themselves a pleasant trip to New York. Also in the party of wives was the Baroness Riedesel, along with the couple's three children.

Although Burgoyne and Gates had agreed to a convention after the surrender of the British that would allow Burgoyne's troops to return home, this was subsequently revoked and his men were taken prisoner.

The citizens of Great Barrington had only just heard of the British surrender to General Gates when Laura Ingersoll's hometown found itself the scene of an encampment for the prisoners of war.

Elizabeth Ingersoll would have been accustomed to the sight and sound of the men of the militia tramping past her Main Street house, as they made their way to and from the various skirmishes. Perhaps she also witnessed, with two-year-old Laura clinging to her skirts, the spectacle of General Burgoyne and thousands of captured British and allied soldiers being led down the main thoroughfare of town.

The American officers and their long line of captives had followed an old trail from Saratoga, New York, through Kinderhook, and down into Great Barrington, where they would camp en route to Virginia and prison.

General Burgoyne would eventually return to England to defend his conduct. He never received the trial he had hoped for, and he was deprived of his regiment. Baron Riedesel, his wife, and their three daughters, along with the army of British and allied troops captured after the Battle of Saratoga, were imprisoned in Charlottesville, Virginia, where they engaged in subsistence farming. The Riedesels were later allowed to move to New York City, and finally, in 1781, they were permitted to journey to Canada and subsequently return home to Germany.

When Washington's army besieged the British under the command of Lord Cornwallis at Yorktown, Virginia, and the French fleet cut off his escape, Cornwallis surrendered in October 1781. He tried to get a promise of protection for those Loyalists who had been part of his army. When that failed, he secured an armed ship for their escape.

Negotiations for peace began. After an eight-year struggle, the Treaty of Paris in 1783 recognized the independence of the United States and set out its boundaries.

Fifteen months after the death of his wife Elizabeth in 1784 and the departure of baby Abigail, Thomas Ingersoll provided his young family with a new mother. On May 26, 1785, he married Mercy Smith, widow of Josiah Smith who had been killed in the American War of Independence.

It was said of Laura's second mother that she taught Thomas's daughters to read and introduced the fine art of needlework and drawing into a home that had been filled with too much sadness. But the joy was to be short-lived. Four years later Mercy would die of tuberculosis, and once again the three Ingersoll girls would be motherless.

Although Massachusetts had, as early as 1647, mandated that every town with a population of more than fifty families support elementary schools, Laura most likely received what education she had at home. One source suggests that Thomas had hoped to send her to a boarding school for young ladies in Boston, one of the few large towns where secondary education was available. No doubt he was aware how quick she was to learn. But by the time Laura might have been of an age to attend a boarding school, conditions in the state were so out of control that it was unwise for her to leave home.

Family members later described Laura Ingersoll as having a fair complexion, dark eyes, and masses of light brown hair. She was a delicate-looking young girl with a slim build. But she was far from fragile. At thirteen, she was already capable of looking after her younger sisters and managing the Ingersoll household in her father's absence, providing direction to the two family servants who tended to the more menial tasks.

Now that the war was over, Thomas, who had risen through the ranks of the state militia, was appointed magistrate upon his return to Great Barrington. There had been no children from his marriage to Mercy Smith, and four months after her death, on September 20, 1789, he married Sarah (Sally) Backus, daughter of Lieutenant Gamaliel Whiting and the sister of General John Whiting. Sally, a widow, already had one daughter, and Harriet quickly became part of the Ingersoll family. At ten, she was the same age as her stepsister Elizabeth.

Sally and Thomas Ingersoll subsequently had seven more children, four boys and three girls. The first, Charles Fortescue, was born in Great Barrington on September 27, 1791. Laura had just turned sixteen.

Although Laura may well have missed Mother Mercy's art instruction, there were new babies to look after, and Sally proved to be a robust and cheerful ally, more like an older sister than a parent.

Times were hard after the war ended. Many people were destitute, and there was no work to be had. The United States was gripped by a severe depression. English merchants were dumping goods in America, but allowing Americans to sell in Britain only those goods the English couldn't get anywhere else.

The colonists' paper money was useless, and even law-abiding citizens were jailed for lack of funds to pay their taxes. The editor of one Massachusetts newspaper, the *Worcester Spy*, accepted salt pork for subscriptions. When Thomas Ingersoll had difficulty collecting the fees due him for his magisterial duties he took feed and grain for his horses as payment. Massachusetts was close to bankruptcy.

Shay's Rebellion, a citizens' revolt against these difficult conditions, broke out in the state in 1786, led by Daniel Shay, a veteran of the war. Thomas helped to put down the rebellion, and it was at this point that he was promoted to the rank of major. Although the revolt had been a failure, it had caused more and more people to recognize the need for stronger government.

The Loyalists, having lost the American War of Independence, found themselves aliens in their own country, with no jobs and their land and possessions confiscated. Those Loyalists who didn't flee the country were at risk of being tortured or even murdered.

With the Treaty of Paris, signed in 1783, the British had been generous to the Americans in terms of settlement, with the understanding that the individual states would return the Loyalists' land or compensate them for it. Congress had no power to force the states to do right by the Loyalists, however, and except in the case of South Carolina, where some compensation was made, it didn't happen. Wagonloads of Loyalist women and children left their homeland, moving north through New York State to find refuge in settlements at Cataraqui (Kingston) or Niagara.

Thomas Ingersoll was disgusted by the continued persecution of the Loyalists after the war was over and the fact that such criminal behaviour went unpunished by the American courts. In better times he had borrowed heavily, hoping to grow his business, but by that time he had realized that no matter how hard he worked, he would never be as prosperous as he once was. He heard there was land available on generous terms in Upper Canada and, deeply in debt, he began to think of leaving the country.

2

Departure for Upper Canada

Prior to the American War of Independence there had been no white settlement west of the Niagara River. By the time that war ended in 1783, the population of Niagara had grown to ten thousand. Those early settlers were the Loyalists, who'd fought on the side of the British and had fled the tyranny of the colonies south of the border. Settlement at that point was largely along a narrow frontier bordering the Niagara River.

In 1791 the Constitutional Act divided the province of Quebec into Upper and Lower Canada. Colonel John Graves Simcoe, once a commander of Loyalist troops himself (the Queen's Rangers) was appointed the first lieutenant-governor of Upper Canada.

Simcoe recognized the need for more settlers if the young province was to thrive. He issued a proclamation inviting Americans to move to Upper Canada — Americans who were British at heart, who were fed up with the lawlessness and corruption that was rampant in the United States at the time — Americans like Thomas Ingersoll. Although some Loyalists and members of his government warned against it, Simcoe was confident that he was on the right track.

Lured by glowing reports of fertile land, abundant forests, and teeming rivers in Canada, Thomas Ingersoll felt ready to return to the pioneering life his ancestors had led 150 years earlier, even if it meant living under British rule again and swearing allegiance to King George III.

About this time, while he was in New York on business, Thomas was introduced to the celebrated chief of the Six Nations, Joseph Brant, who along with his sister Molly Johnson, had persuaded his people to fight on the side of the British in the American War of Independence. Chief Brant had already selected land along the Grand River in Upper Canada as a home for the Six Nations people, and he offered, if and when Thomas came to Canada, to show him the best place for a settlement.

Thomas Ingersoll and four associates, including the Reverend Gideon Bostwick of Great Barrington, Massachusetts, drew up the necessary petition asking Lieutenant-Governor Simcoe for a township grant in Upper Canada. In order to present the petition in person, Thomas, as the group's representative, journeyed in March 1793 to Newark (the name Simcoe gave Niagara, today's Niagara-on-the-Lake), which was then the seat of government for Upper Canada.

Two months later, the government granted Thomas and his associates sixty-six thousand acres (twenty-seven thousand hectares) of land. The township chosen was in the Thames Valley, and the new settlement was to be called Oxford-on-the-Thames. It is today the site of the town of Ingersoll, near London, Ontario.

It is possible that Laura, then almost eighteen, accompanied her father on an initial journey to Upper Canada to see for herself their future home, before making the trek with the whole family. She was accustomed to helping Thomas with his business accounts, and it seems reasonable that he would seek the approval of his trusted eldest child on this latest, and boldest, enterprise.

If she did go with him on one of his early expeditions, Laura may have been able to allay the fears back home somewhat. What would life be like in a new country where the Ingersolls would suddenly be thrust into the role of pioneers and farmers?

At the very least, Laura could assure the younger ones that their father would be with them in their new home, not away fighting wars or tending to his magisterial duties.

As he'd promised, Chief Joseph Brant sent six of his men to escort Thomas through the woods to show him the choicest piece of property, where there was already a small clearing, once part of a Native summer camping ground.

In return for the land grant the petitioners agreed to bring forty additional families to the township within seven years. Each of those families would receive two hundred acres (eighty-one hectares) for the nominal fee of sixpence per acre. Within one year of the date of the assignment, they would be expected to make improvements on their land, which included clearing five acres, beginning cultivation, building a house, and opening a road across the front of the property.

The remainder of the sixty-six thousand acres that comprised the township was to be held in trust by Thomas Ingersoll and Associates to be sold at the same price. Unfortunately, Gideon Bostwick, one of the four members of the group of petitioners, died just three months after the petition was granted.

It was another two years before Thomas could wind up his business affairs and sell the family home in Great Barrington. Laura's name appears as a witness on a document for the sale of some of her father's property as early as January 11, 1793. Her signature appears again on documents dated April 21, 1795, in which she witnessed the relinquishment of her stepmother, Sally Backus Ingersoll, to her rights in her husband's property.

Laura Ingersoll was nearly twenty when the time came to move to Upper Canada. No doubt she had a hand in choosing the few possessions the family could take with them and helping to dispose of the rest. A large chest packed with clothing, bedding, and some of the fine china and glassware, the mantel clock, Betsy's rocking chair, and the four-poster bed would go on ahead. There was much preparation for the long and arduous journey they were about to embark on. For one family that made the same trek seven years after the Ingersolls had, the journey reportedly took an entire month.

Two more babies had been born since Laura's father decided to leave the country — Charlotte in 1793 and Appolonia (Appy) in April the following year.

The first part of their journey took the Ingersolls and all their bundles by wagon, west to the Hudson River. They may have stayed overnight along the way at the home of a relative or at an inn, and the next day they boarded a small boat for the sail up the Hudson to Albany, New York. From there it was overland again by wagon, ten miles to Schenectady. Ahead was the one-hundred-mile trip north on the Mohawk River in a Durham boat.

Durham boats — large, flat-bottomed vessels with high vertical sides — were mainly used to transport freight because they could carry heavy loads and displaced very little water. They were powered by a small crew, two on each side, that walked back and forth on "walking boards" built into the sides of the boat, either rowing or using ten-foot-long, iron-tipped "setting poles" to move the boat along. If the boat were going downstream, the poles could be used to steer it, but if it were going upstream, as it was on the Ingersolls' trip on the Mohawk, the poles were used to push the boat against the swift current.

After a portage — and there was a total of thirty miles of portages — the family crossed Oneida Lake and travelled up the Oswego River to the southeastern shore of Lake Ontario.

There, at the port of Oswego, the Ingersolls boarded a schooner for the final voyage to Upper Canada. It must have been a relief for everyone to know this was the last leg of their journey. Four-year-old Charles may well have been pestering his parents and older sisters long before this with questions of "Are we there yet?" and "How much farther is it?" And little Charlotte would be delighted now to have space to toddle about on this larger vessel.

At some point during the crossing, after an ominous calm that had emptied the ship's sails, a violent thunderstorm struck the lake. High winds whipped up huge waves and tossed the vessel about like a toy boat. Everyone feared the ship would capsize. The children were crying and many passengers were seasick by the time the captain managed to get the ship into a sheltered bay, where they could wait out the storm.

Laura would have been among the first to comfort the little ones and assure them that the worst was over. Or was it? Provisions were running low on the ship and too lengthy a delay would cause more suffering, especially to the youngest passengers, and to Sally, who was expecting another baby.

The captain put some of the crew ashore to try to find enough food to last for the rest of the voyage. Fortunately, the sailors encountered a group of hunters who directed them to the home of a lone settler willing to share what he had. The men returned to the ship with bread and milk for everyone, and when they were able to set sail again, the remainder of the journey went smoothly.

It isn't known exactly where the Ingersoll family disembarked in Upper Canada, but it was likely that the ship docked at either Niagara or Queenston. Sally and the young Ingersolls would have been relieved that Thomas had arranged for their accommodation at an inn in the town. Once he saw that they were comfortable, Thomas continued on to the Thames Valley to claim his land and to make sure that the family's furniture that had been sent ahead had arrived.

Before any settlement was possible, the township had first to be surveyed and roads had to be built. While he waited for this to be accomplished, Thomas Ingersoll took over the operation of a tavern back in Queenston, returning whenever he could to his property to work on the log house he was building for the family and to clear more of the land.

The bustling town of Queenston, also called "The Landing," was an ideal place to run a business. It was at the northern end of the Portage Road that had been built to bypass the rapids in the Niagara River and Niagara Falls. Merchandise and food such as salt pork and flour moved in one direction over the portage, and furs from the upper Great Lakes travelled along the same route in the opposite direction.

Niagara (Newark) was the area's social and military centre, but Queenston was the head of navigation. Every day a long line of wagons could be seen waiting for freight to be unloaded off boats from York, Kingston, or Montreal that had docked at the busy Queenston wharf. Drawn by teams of horses or oxen, the wagons would then transport the goods along the Portage Road to Chippawa, three miles beyond the falls.

Queenston had been founded to provide a port on the western side of the Niagara River after the treaty that ended the American Revolution gave the eastern side to the United States.

The town's founder was Scottish-born merchant Robert Hamilton, who was instrumental in the building of the Portage Road. In 1780, Hamilton went into partnership as a shipping agent with Richard Cartwright at Niagara, and there they established a firm trade with the British army and the Indian Department. Although Cartwright established himself in Kingston in 1785, their partnership continued until the end of the decade.

After the American War of Independence, the fur traders in Montreal gave the business of portaging their goods on the west side of the Niagara River to Robert Hamilton. Around 1785 he built a house and a shop at what would one day become Queenston. The two-storey Georgian mansion built of stone sat high on the Niagara Escarpment and overlooked the village on one side and the river and the American shore on another. Over the years, Hamilton and his wife entertained many visiting dignitaries at their impressive home.

The wealthy Hamilton was Queenston's most prominent citizen and the biggest landowner. He owned a distillery and a tannery in the village and was involved in other businesses both there and in Chippawa. A leading public figure in the Niagara district, he was appointed by Lieutenant-Governor Simcoe to the first Legislative Council of Upper Canada. Even up until the time of his death in 1809, Hamilton held military contracts with the British to supply and carry provisions to their upper posts at Detroit and Michilimackinac.

—//—

Thomas Ingersoll hired his wife Sally's brother, Charles Whiting, to survey his township, and Whiting began to lay out concessions and sideroads using Thomas's log house on Lot 20 as the base for his work. Thomas himself built the settlement's first road. Today there are two creeks in the area named Ingersoll and Whiting, in honour of these pioneers.

In October 1796, as soon as the survey was complete, other settlers began to arrive and at once started to clear their land. Brush was burned, log homes built, and the land between trees too large to take down was cultivated.

For the first couple of years in Upper Canada the tavern in Queenston provided Thomas a roof over his family's head and a means to support them. Taverns were an important part of life in those early days and were often family-run enterprises. Not only did these establishments offer food and drink, they also provided rooms for weary travellers and were regular meeting places for the community. The Ingersoll Tavern in Queenston, most likely located on the south side of the landing, was occasionally used for meetings of an early Masonic lodge, and in 1796 Thomas himself became a Mason.

Operating the tavern gave the Ingersoll family the opportunity to meet many people in the Niagara region, and they soon became well-known and respected. Every Ingersoll old enough to help out worked at the tavern, particularly the older girls. Their father was often out of town, either building the log house or on one of his trips to the United States, where he continued to work at persuading more Americans to move to Upper Canada.

Late in 1796, Thomas was finally able to move his family into the log house at Oxford-on-the-Thames.

—//—

Under Lieutenant-Governor Simcoe's plan, the government of Upper Canada made land grants of whole townships available, but the conditions of the grant had always been a little fuzzy. Early on, Thomas was dismayed to learn that he might never receive clear title to his land.

Some locals were suspicious of the politics of American settlers like Thomas Ingersoll, calling the newcomers to the province "late Loyalists." Representations were made to the government suggesting these settlers might actually do more harm to the country than good. Thomas and his settlement of close to ninety families suddenly found themselves facing an uncertain future.

Government policy changed after Simcoe's term was over and he returned to England in 1796. Arrangements had already been made to bring a thousand settlers up from New York, when growing opposition to Simcoe's plan resulted in its being phased out.

No longer would whole townships be granted, and Thomas's contract was cancelled. The reason given for this action was that he hadn't fulfilled his part of the agreement. Although he *had* delivered the required number of settlers, he had run out of money for the building of roads in the township.

To have the settlement taken away in this manner, after the years he had spent working on it, seemed grossly unfair, and, understandably, Thomas Ingersoll felt he had been cheated. He had staked his entire personal fortune on Oxford-on-the-Thames. Although he had been appointed justice of the peace while he lived there, he abandoned the settlement in 1805 and moved his family to the Credit River.

In his new location ten miles west of York (Toronto), Thomas signed a seven-year lease to operate an inn called Government House. The inn had originally been built by the government of Upper Canada to accommodate judges and other government officials having business at York. The town was a long way from anywhere in those days.

When war between Britain and France had broken out in 1793, Lieutenant-Governor Simcoe had been faced with the possibility of an American attack on Upper Canada, France having been an ally of the Americans in the War of Independence. Simcoe established a naval base at York, and on February 1, 1796, the capital of Upper Canada was moved to York, a less vulnerable location than Newark had been.

In the Ingersolls' day, many travellers found a warm welcome at Government House, whether they came by horse or stagecoach, or by boat on Lake Ontario or the Credit River. In return, the inn gave the Ingersoll family a comfortable living, and with the help of his wife and children, Thomas ran the establishment until his death in 1812 at the age of sixty-three.

Thomas and Sally Ingersoll's son James, who was born in 1801, had been the first white child born in Oxford-on-the-Thames. He was four years old when the family moved to the Credit River. His sister, Sarah, was yet to be born. She would arrive in 1807, the last child for Thomas and Sally Ingersoll.

After Thomas died, his widow Sally and their eldest son, Charles, applied to renew the lease on the inn. Because Charles was by that time involved in the War of 1812, Sally operated the inn herself. Later the Ingersolls moved from the Credit River, although Sally continued to live there until her death in 1833.

In a stroke of irony, in 1817 Charles purchased, at a sheriff's sale, his father's old farm in Oxford-on-the-Thames. He and his younger brother Thomas, born in 1796 most likely at Queenston, built a new house there, as well as a sawmill, gristmill, store, potashery, and a distillery. They called the new village "Ingersoll" in honour of their father.

Charles moved his own family to Ingersoll from Queenston in 1821. He became a magistrate and was the first postmaster of Ingersoll, succeeded in that position by his younger brother James.

In 1834, Charles was a commissioner in the Court of Request. As well as being appointed lieutenant colonel of the 2nd Oxford Militia, he was a Member of the Canadian Parliament in 1824, and was twice returned, in 1829 and 1832. Charles Ingersoll died of cholera in 1832, at the same time as his eldest son.

James Ingersoll died August 9, 1886, at the age of eighty-six. For over forty years he had been Registrar of Oxford County.

Thomas would have been proud.

3

James Secord, United Empire Loyalist

Laura was not with the Ingersoll family when Thomas pulled up stakes and moved Sally and the children to the Credit River in 1805. Nor had she gone with them in 1796 when they first left Queenston for the log house in the settlement of Oxford-on-the-Thames. Laura had remained behind because she'd met a handsome young man by the name of James Secord and fallen in love.

William Kirby, in his book *Annals of Niagara* (1896), listed among the ladies who stood out in Niagara Society from 1792–1800, "belles of the day," one "Miss Ingersoll." No doubt this was Laura, the eldest of the Ingersoll girls.

She was an attractive twenty-one-year-old in 1796 and part of the area's social scene, with frequent invitations to people's homes, community functions, dances, and parties.

James Secord, who had become a Freemason in 1795 when he was twenty-two, often came into the Ingersoll Tavern in

Queenston. James was the youngest son of one of the most prosperous and well-respected families in the area. The Secords were shopkeepers in nearby St. Davids, a village whose original name had been Four Mile Creek. A number of major creeks in the area were named according to their distance from the Niagara River.

Much of the stock for Secord's store would arrive by ship at Queenston, and occasionally James would be the one to come to the landing to collect the shipment. A stop at the Ingersoll Tavern before heading back seemed to be in order for the young man who had been immediately attracted to the vivacious girl with the expressive brown eyes — Laura Ingersoll, daughter of the owner.

James Secord had been born in New Rochelle, in the colony of New York, on July 7, 1773. His parents were James Secord Sr. and Madelaine Badeau. He'd been just five years old when he and his family came to Niagara from the United States in 1778. His father, Lieutenant James Secord Sr., and two older brothers were members of Butler's Rangers, among the first Loyalists to come to Upper Canada.

Organized by Colonel John Butler, the Rangers had fought on the side of the British during the American War of Independence. Colonel Butler had been aware that many Loyalists who had tried to return home after the war had been either banished, thrown in prison, or murdered, and he arranged for his Rangers and their families to have a home on the west side of the Niagara River.

Another account has Mrs. Secord and four other women, accompanied by thirty-one children, including James, arriving by wagon at Fort Niagara "in a starving state."

The group had fled through the wilderness, escaping for their lives from a band of ruffians who were intent on driving Loyalists from their homes on the banks of the Hudson

River and the Mohawk Valley. After nearly a month of hardship the refugees, guided on the journey by friendly Natives of the Iroquois Confederacy, arrived at Fort Niagara with only the clothes on their backs.

Land grants were made to Butler's Rangers around 1784, after the lots had been surveyed. Until then, all new arrivals squatted close to Fort Niagara, where they were given tents, food, and clothing. Nearly everyone had to depend on the generosity of the government. The food rations they received consisted of flour, pork, a limited amount of beef, and a bit of butter. For a period of three years, or until they could provide clothing for themselves, the refugees were supplied with coarse cloth to make their own trousers and dresses, with Indian blankets to be made into warm coats, and with shoes.

Once they received their land grant the Loyalists were given some basic tools, some seed grain to cultivate, and possibly a cow that they would share with one other family. As well, the government saw that gristmills were shortly erected to aid the settlers.

However he got there, James Secord grew up on the Niagara Peninsula, and at the time of his meeting with Laura Ingersoll, he owned two hundred acres at St. Davids, land he'd received as a United Empire Loyalist.

The Secord family came originally from La Rochelle, France, where their name was D'Secor (or Sicard). One of the men in the family had converted to Protestantism and his descendants followed suit. Those of that particular branch of the family who survived the persecution of the French Huguenots (French Protestants) in the sixteenth and seventeenth centuries included five brothers who eventually immigrated to America, settling in Westchester County, New York. They founded the town of New Rochelle and became successful lumbermen.

When the American War of Independence divided the family's loyalty, those who sided with the British changed their surname to the more anglicized *Secord*.

Although the exact date and location of Laura Ingersoll's wedding to James Secord is not known, it was most likely in June 1797. The marriage records have been lost. The couple may well have been married by James's older brother, David, who was a justice of the peace in St. Davids. All his records were lost when the town was burned by the Americans in July 1814.

Only clergymen of the Church of England (Anglican) were permitted to perform weddings at the time. Except for circuit riders or saddlebag preachers, clergy in Upper Canada were scarce. For this reason, magistrates were commonly called upon to perform marriage ceremonies.

Because James Secord's family was wealthy, one can imagine that the wedding of Laura and James would have been quite lavish, complete with ribbon-tied, handwritten invitations. Had Laura's family come from Oxford-on-the-Thames to attend the happy event? Her sisters Elizabeth and Mira were young adults of seventeen and fifteen respectively. The Ingersolls' daughter was marrying well, and it seems likely that Thomas and Laura's stepmother, Sally, would have been there to give the young couple their blessing.

It was usual at that time for the wedding ceremony to be held in the evening and for the bride to wear white, with "something borrowed" for good luck. It was customary for the groom's parents to give an elaborate supper for the many guests, and this would be followed by dancing — or cards for those who desired a less strenuous activity.

After the wedding, Laura went to live in the house in St. Davids that had been built for James. The front half of the ground floor of the house was taken up by James's store; the merchandise — everything from bolts of printed calico, pudding dishes, and brass candlesticks to casks of rum, men's hats, and snuff boxes — was displayed in the front windows so that people passing by in the street could see what was for sale. The rest of the house was their private home.

Laura would have been a willing and capable assistant in James's store, accustomed to helping her father Thomas in his business, and the tiny community of St. Davids, four miles west of Queenston, welcomed the shy new bride into their midst. Laura's closest friend and confidante in the village was her sister-in-law, Hannah (or Annatie) DeFreest Secord, wife of Stephen (or Etienne). The Stephen Secords lived at the northeast end of the village, where they ran a mill.

Hannah may well have been at Laura's bedside to assist her when she delivered her first child, Mary, born in St. Davids in 1799.

More than anything, James wanted to provide Laura with many luxuries, but he'd fallen into the habit of extending credit to his customers and was having trouble getting paid enough to make ends meet. During the early years of the Secords' marriage, finances were often strained.

Hoping to remedy the situation, James made the decision to establish a general store in Queenston, a much more important centre of business than little St. Davids. He opened the store near the wharf in Queenston and bought land near what was then the end of town, below the Niagara Escarpment, a short walk from his business. There he would one day build a house for his family.

In the meantime, he commuted between Queenston and their home in St. Davids. Daughter Charlotte arrived in 1801, and two years later, on February 10, 1803, Harriet was born.

Source: Wikipedia. Author Ken Lund.

The restored Secord home at Queenston, now an interpretive centre.

Richard Cartwright (1759–1815), the husband of James's only sister, Magdalene, was one of the most successful businessmen in Upper Canada. He became James Secord's adviser. He was also James's chief supplier of goods for his store.

Based at Niagara, Cartwright, a committed Loyalist, had served as secretary for John Butler's Rangers until 1780. Subsequently, he became a merchant involved in the provisioning trade and was for ten years in partnership with the wealthy shipping agent Robert Hamilton, the founder of Queenston.

After moving to Kingston in 1785, Cartwright built up the largest retail outlet in the town. As well as being a justice of the peace and a judge in the Court of Common Pleas, he was a member of the first Legislative Council of Upper Canada. Before Simcoe returned to England, he commissioned Cartwright lieutenant-governor of Frontenac County.

James Secord had the idea that he would like to establish a potashery. Potash was first produced when the settlers were clearing their land and burning the hardwood trees. The product was obtained by leaching the ashes left from the fire and then catching the runoff to be evaporated in iron pots.

The result was caustic potash, which the settlers used to make soap. The sale of wood ashes to the Americans had provided Canadian settlers with easy cash. In fact, potash had been exported from Canada from as early as 1767, sent to England for the fledgling chemical industry.

It was Richard Cartwright's opinion that his brother-in-law James Secord took too many risks. Operating a business in Upper Canada wasn't easy, particularly when people often had to resort to paying for their purchases with goods instead of cash.

Although not the best businessman in the world, even with Laura's help, James was hardworking and honest. He was also by then deeply in debt. He owed his brother-in-law Richard money, and he was also in debt to the prominent merchants the McGill Brothers of Montreal. The McGills had business connections to Richard Cartwright, and Richard was urging James to pay them off. At some point Richard even took over some of James's debt to the McGills, on top of what James already owed him.

In 1801, James mortgaged his farm in St. Davids to Richard so that his creditors could be paid. That same year Laura appeared before a judge in Niagara, signing away her "claim of dower" on any of their property.

Sometime after Harriet's birth in 1803, James thought he could see better times ahead, and he moved his family into their new house in Queenston. The white frame house of one and a half storeys with two small rooms upstairs sat below the escarpment that rose above the village to Queenston Heights.

That first winter in Queenston was long and very cold. Many days it was impossible for the residents of the town to leave their homes. Laura would have been thankful that she'd had the foresight to dry the berries she'd picked the previous summer, along with some of the garden vegetables and the peaches and apples from the orchards in St. Davids. She was fortunate to live in the best fruit-growing area in Upper Canada, on the south shore of Lake Ontario, between the Niagara River and the head of the lake. The first settlers to the region, the Loyalists, had planted cuttings they'd brought from the fruit trees they had left behind in the Mohawk Valley and Pennsylvania.

Tucked away in the kitchen dresser, the seeds Laura had saved from last year's beans, squash, and corn would be the genesis of her new garden in Queenston in the spring. For now, she and her three little daughters could only stare out at the snow piling up in the yard.

Soon, two more babies would join the family — the couple's only son, Charles Badeau, was born in 1809, and a fourth daughter, Appolonia (Appy), arrived in 1810.

James was now a wholesaler in flour, potash, and other goods. In 1810, when his business needed an infusion of cash, he and Laura sold 228 acres of land in Nelson (now Burlington), part of her inheritance from her father.

As the years passed, James's business picked up. With Britain and Napoleonic France again at war, his main concern was that the sea lanes stay open so that he could get his supplies from England.

Laura had always admired her husband's optimism, the way he kept his spirits up, sure of better days ahead. She knew they might never be out of debt, but life was good. Their five children were healthy, happy youngsters, and she and James loved each other. Years later, their daughter Harriet wrote that her parents had always been "most devoted to each other and lived in the closest mutual affection."

The Secords' lives weren't without sorrow, but they had much to be thankful for. Laura's beloved sisters had all married, although Elizabeth, who had married Reverend Daniel Pickett in 1806, had died in 1811. Mira was married to Julius Hitchcock, and the family had received the good news that little Abigail, the sister who had been adopted by the Nashes, had married Guy Woodsworth in 1804 and had moved with him to Vermont.

Early in 1812, Laura received word from Port Credit that her father, Thomas Ingersoll, had had a stroke and was asking for her. She hurried to his bedside as quickly as possible and he died the following day.

By 1812, James Secord was able to write in a letter that he was "in easy circumstances." His house was modest but comfortable. He and Laura had two black servants, and James had managed to pick up several pieces of property that he hoped to sell at a profit.

Back in 1792, when John Graves Simcoe arrived as the first lieutenant-governor of Upper Canada, there had been seven hundred blacks living in the province. Most of them had been slaves who had arrived after the American War of Independence as spoils of war, or those that had belonged to the Loyalists.

Simcoe's *Act Against Slavery*, passed July 7, 1793, had banned further importation of slaves and granted gradual emancipation to those born in the province. It did not abolish slavery altogether, which is what Simcoe had desired, but it was, however, the first act to limit slavery in the British Empire.

It was not uncommon in Upper Canada for successful merchants like James Secord to have black servants. He and Laura had two: a girl named Fan (or Floss) and a man whose name was Bob. They were no longer slaves, but rather paid employees, and they were treated with respect by everyone in the family.

After her years in St. Davids, where several of her neighbours were also her in-laws, Laura was now less shy than she had been. She had become part of the social life in the busy town of Queenston, attending Sunday church services, taking part in spinning and sewing circles, visiting friends, and chatting over afternoon tea.

When Simcoe arrived in 1792, British troops still occupied the forts at Michilimackinac, Detroit, Oswego, and Niagara — that refuge of Loyalists and Indians from the American War of Independence. These old wooden forts, many of them in a state of disrepair, were on the American side of the frontier that had been set by the Treaty of Paris in 1783. By rights, the British should have returned them. Britain argued that the Americans themselves had not fulfilled all the terms of the treaty, but because she was again at war with France, Britain was not eager to get into another war with the Americans over the issue.

The Jay Treaty in 1794 provided for the British to leave the forts by June 1, 1796. When that day came, the British troops moved back across the lakes and rivers and the American troops took over.

In 1806, James Monroe, former American ambassador to France and, at the time, minister to the Court of St. James, negotiated a treaty with Britain to replace the Jay Treaty. The American president, Thomas Jefferson, rejected it in 1807 because it contained no ban on Britain's infuriating practice of conscripting American sailors, referred to as "impressment."

Britain had found that it was losing sailors when they jumped ship upon docking in the United States. Consequently, Britain declared its right to stop and search neutral American ships at sea for deserters and to conscript sailors, even though they might be American citizens.

Some politicians in Washington wanted Britain out of North America altogether and the whole of the Great Lakes region brought under the American flag. Although the northern states didn't want war with Canada, the "war hawks" in Congress demanded that President James Madison, who had succeeded Jefferson, declare war.

There would be no need to fight the war in England; Canada was right there for the taking. With Britain occupied in Europe in the war with France, it should be an easy victory. There were 7.5 million Americans and a trained army of thirty-five thousand, compared to only half a million British subjects in Canada. And one-fifth of those were "late Loyalists," who could go either way. At best, the Canadas had five thousand British soldiers and possibly four thousand militia. Arms, too, were in short supply.

By the summer of 1811 the crisis had reached the boiling point. Citizens in the United States were talking openly about annexing Canada, and there were some Canadians who welcomed the idea.

Perhaps, while she sat sewing with her friends or visiting the shops in Queenston, Laura heard such rumblings from those in the community who were American sympathizers. Certainly everyone was talking about the possibility of an American invasion. It seemed only a question of when.

The Loyalist militia in the Niagara Peninsula had begun to drill. Another war was on her doorstep, and before it was over, Laura's whole life would be changed.

4

Isaac Brock and the Battle of Queenston Heights

James Secord, who had earlier held the rank of captain in the First Lincoln County Militia, had resigned, as much over a business issue as over a disagreement he'd had with a senior officer. But now, with war threatening, he rejoined his old regiment as a sergeant in Captain Isaac Swayze's unit of Provincial Artillery Drivers — the Car Brigade that used farm horses to move the field guns during battle.

Because Britain's regular troops were busy fighting Napoleon in Europe — in that long war that except for a few short periods lasted from 1792 to 1815 — the number of British soldiers in Upper Canada was small. Every able-bodied man in the province between the ages of sixteen and sixty was being recruited, and this ragtag militia was being whipped into shape by Isaac Brock, commander of the British forces in Upper Canada.

Isaac Brock had been born into a well-to-do family in 1769 on the island of Guernsey, one of England's Channel Islands. When he was fifteen he joined the British army as a junior officer. In 1795 he joined the 49th Regiment of Foot, and in 1797 Lieutenant Colonel Brock became its commander.

In 1802, Brock and his regiment were sent to Canada to strengthen British defences there. It was thought that the Americans might choose to attack Canada while British troops were busy fighting in Europe.

During the three-year-long stay of the 49th at York, Brock familiarized himself with the territory he might be called upon to defend — a vast frontier that stretched from Cornwall to Michilimackinac. It was obvious to the young commander that the defence of Upper Canada was going to have to depend on its inhabitants, most of whom were farmers.

Brock was also concerned about the loyalty of the people of Upper Canada, many of whom he said believed that "the province must inevitably succumb." Many Canadians had friends and family still living on the other side of the border and might welcome annexation to the United States.

In 1805, Brock became a colonel and was temporarily put in charge of all the forces in the Canadas until a new commander-in-chief arrived in 1807. Later that year he was promoted to brigadier general, and in the summer of 1810 he took command of the troops in Upper Canada.

Brock was also given the job of political administrator of Upper Canada when Lieutenant-Governor Francis Gore took a leave of absence in England, where he would stay until the war was over.

Isaac Brock, who was well-loved and respected by his men, had now reached the rank of major general. A tall, blond, imposing figure, he had other interests besides the military. The expert horseman was also a sociable person who enjoyed dinner parties and dancing. He loved to read the epic stories of Greek heroes and could speak fluent French.

As the tension between Britain and the United States increased, Brock kept asking for more troops and supplies from Commander-in-Chief George Prevost in Quebec. He also tried to convince the legislature of Upper Canada that they must prepare for war.

Faced with leaders who felt any military effort was doomed to failure, with Prevost who really didn't want to upset the Americans, and with a force of only 1,500 regulars spread out from Kingston to Fort Amherstburg on the Detroit River, Brock turned for help from Britain's allies, the Indians.

After being driven from their homelands northwest of New England, the Indians had declared the Americans their sworn enemies. In spite of Native resistance, thousands of American settlers began moving into the area south of Lake Erie and north of the Ohio River. Brock sympathized with the plight of the Native people and believed that all of the area known as Michigan Territory should belong to them.

Although Prevost disagreed with it, Brock's strategy was to strike first at the Americans in the west. He sent a letter to Robert Dickson, a Scotsman who ran a trading post at Lake Traverse and who had lived amongst the Sioux Nation. Dickson had married a Sioux woman and had learned the language and customs of the Native people, gaining their trust. In his letter, Brock asked for their support in the area of Michilimackinac where there was a fort held by the Americans. Whoever held the fort controlled the straits between Lake Huron and Lake Michigan and, ultimately, the fur trade. Naturally, Brock wanted it back in British hands.

Although Prevost had given his reluctant consent to the defence of Upper Canada, he had ordered Brock to wait until the Americans made the first move.

On June 18, 1812, the United States declared war against Great Britain, and Brock sent orders to Captain Charles Roberts, who commanded St. Joseph's Island near Michilimackinac, to attack the fort. Dickson had 130 Native warriors at the ready, waiting for orders from Captain Roberts.

The Americans at Fort Michilimackinac had not yet heard about the declaration of war, and when Roberts attacked on July 17 they were taken by surprise and surrendered at once, with no loss of life.

This early victory for the British, Canadian, and Native forces resulted in many more volunteers coming forward to join the militia and, in the eyes of the Native people, Brock was regarded as a victorious warrior. With the capture of Fort Michilimackinac, the British were able to hold the Midwest for the rest of the war. After the peace treaty was signed late in 1814, Fort Michilimackinac would be returned to the United States.

When Tecumseh, the famous Shawnee war chief, heard how Brock had defeated the Americans in the first battle of the war, he led hundreds of his warriors north to be of assistance.

On July 25, American forces led by Brigadier General William Hull crossed the river from Fort Detroit to invade Canada, occupying Sandwich (now Windsor) above Fort Amherstburg.

Brock was at York in a meeting of the legislature when he heard about Hull's invasion of Canada. Expecting that the Americans' next move would be to try to take Fort Amherstburg at the northwest end of Lake Erie, he sent Colonel Henry Proctor to take command.

As soon as possible, Brock left York with his troops and

headed for Amherstburg himself, travelling the length of Lake Erie, into the teeth of the wind and rain that swept across the water. When Hull heard that Brock was coming he retreated to the safety of the stockade at Fort Detroit, at the gateway to Michigan Territory.

Across the river at Fort Amherstburg, Brock and Tecumseh met to develop their plan of attack. When all was ready, Brock advanced on Detroit and demanded General Hull surrender the fort. He let Hull know that if he didn't surrender, Brock couldn't be responsible for the behaviour of his Native troops. The idea of Native warriors running amok in Detroit frightened General Hull.

While Brock waited for Hull's reply to his demand for surrender, he marched a handful of his regulars, the militia who were also dressed in discarded British uniforms, and Tecumseh's braves back and forth, crossing and re-crossing the same trails where they were visible to the troops holding Fort Detroit across the river. This bit of theatre made it appear as if Brock had twice the number of professional troops and a much larger Native force at his disposal.

Earlier in the week, under cover of darkness, Brock's men had set up a battery in a grove of trees opposite the fort. When Hull's reply came that he would not surrender, in the night the trees that hid the battery were cut down. The next day, August 16, 1812, Brock's men crossed the Detroit River and began the march toward the fort. One source states that the first shot in the War of 1812 was fired from the battery on the Canadian side, slamming into Fort Detroit.

Hull's guns returned the fire, and for a while shots flew back and forth across the river. Only after an 18-pound British shell shattered the officers' mess, killing four men, did Hull surrender.

By taking Fort Detroit, and with it most of the Michigan Territory, the militia and the government of Upper Canada felt more confident of success. The victorious British forces took hundreds of prisoners as well as a cache of much-needed weapons and supplies.

The American prisoners of war were sent in groups to Quebec, some going by warship from York to Kingston, some in small boats along the shore of Lake Ontario and across the Carrying Place portage to the Bay of Quinte. Most of them were kept prisoner in old ships docked at Quebec that were no longer seaworthy, until they could be exchanged.

William Hull was court martialled for cowardice. He said in his defence that he truly believed he had saved Detroit from a massacre at the hands of the Natives. He was subsequently pardoned, but never recovered from his disgrace.

The news that war had been declared had taken some time to spread. Communication moved slowly in those days over the vast distances it had to travel. Once the grim news reached them, many people living along the border moved farther into the interior. With the men gone, those women who decided to stay in their homes, Laura Ingersoll Secord among them, hid their valuables and made sure they had enough provisions to feed their families until the conflict was over. One American newspaper reported that in the towns of Newark and Queenston there were no inhabitants left, except for a few civilians and the soldiers.

Canadians rallied around the hero, Isaac Brock. Lieutenant John Norton, the half-Scottish, half-Cherokee adopted nephew of Chief Joseph Brant, and his Grand River Indians had previously been neutral, but now they threw their support behind the British.

Then came the news that Governor General Prevost had negotiated a one-month ceasefire with the Americans. Brock, who had hoped to keep the momentum going, was bitterly disappointed. He judged that, as soon as the ceasefire ended, the next attack by the American forces would come at the province's most vulnerable point, along the Niagara River. Although the British troops would be outnumbered, Brock figured they would have the advantage because the Americans had first to get across the river with its treacherous cross-currents.

As Brock suspected they would, the Americans used the period of the ceasefire to rally thousands of troops, and now they were heading for the border at the Niagara River.

The British had built a redan — a V-shaped, two-sided military structure — halfway up the Heights above the village of Queenston to house an 18-pound cannon. The big gun was powerful enough to reach Lewiston, on the American side of the river.

In the early morning hours of October 13, while Isaac Brock was at his headquarters at Fort George in Niagara trying to get some much-needed sleep, the Americans crossed the river to attack Queenston. The sound of the big gun at Vrooman's Point, one mile downriver from Queenston, sent Brock leaping from his bed. *Had the assault begun?*

He ran for his horse, Alfred, shouting orders that were to be relayed to his aide-de-camp, Lieutenant Colonel John Macdonell, and to Major John B. Glegg: "I'm off to Queenston. Tell them to follow at all speed."

Fifty of his own 49th Regiment, led by James Dennis, were firing down on the Americans trying to board boats at Lewiston and come across the river. Some American troops had already landed before they'd been spotted by the sentries at Queenston. Hit by gunshot from the Canadian side, a number of American soldiers toppled, dead, into the water. A couple of their boats were caught in the eddies, capsized, and were carried away by the strong current.

Things had not gone smoothly for the Americans. It was not mandatory that the New York State Militia fight outside the country, and many had refused to cross the river. Although they had been expecting at least thirty boats to ferry them across to Queenston, at the point where the river was at its narrowest, only twelve small boats had been made available.

But still the troops kept coming, while more waited on the shore for the boats to return for them to make the crossing. They landed at the Queenston wharf and hunkered under the steep bank at the edge of the river, led by twenty-eight-year-old Captain John Wool. Wool was filling in for his commander, Colonel Solomon van Rensselaer, who had been wounded on landing. One source says Van Rensselaer was wounded five times that day, but survived. The Americans managed to move up the bank, heading for Queenston Heights on the south side of the village.

Meanwhile, Brock raced along the road to Queenston, telling each of the militia units he'd earlier called up in order to patrol the river to follow him. He reined in his big grey horse at Brown's Point just long enough to give the same command to the company of York militia that was guarding the cannon there. "Push on, York Volunteers!" was his rallying cry.

One of the men manning the 24-pound gun at Vrooman's Point called out as Brock passed, "The Americans are crossing the river in force, sir."

Brock believed Queenston Heights was the key to holding Upper Canada. If it fell, so too would the rest of the province.

When he reached Queenston, Brock ordered some of the men manning the battery on the Heights to come down to assist the troops in the village in a effort to stem the flow of American soldiers. When he rode up to the battery himself, intending to get a view of the situation down at the river, bullets rained down around him. To his horror he discovered that the Americans were already on the Heights, above the redan. Led by Captain Wool, they had found an old fisherman's trail that the British had considered to be impassable.

Brock ordered the big gun at the redan spiked to render it useless to the enemy, and he and his men hurried back down to the village where he could rally his troops.

By 9:00 a.m. the British were ready to advance. Never one to send his men where he would not go himself, Brock led his own 49th Regiment and the Lincoln County Militia in a charge up the hill, keeping to the right of the battery, determined to recapture the cannon. He received a shot in his wrist early on the ascent, but ignored it and continued in the lead, brandishing his sword.

Suddenly, an American rifleman stepped out from behind a tree, took aim, and shot Brock in the chest. Major General Isaac Brock made an easy target — a tall British officer, wearing a cockaded hat and scarlet jacket with gold epaulettes. He died almost instantly.

With their commander down, Brock's men began to fall back until his aide-de-camp, Lieutenant Colonel John Macdonell, urged them on. By this time, some of the York Militia who Brock had summoned from Brown's Point had arrived, and along with the 49th Foot led by Captain John Williams made a second attack, charging up the hill, thirsty now to avenge their charismatic commander.

Tragically, Macdonell's horse was shot out from under him, and the young officer was shot in the back as he fell. The British and Canadians retreated down the hill, bearing their dead and wounded. They carried Brock's body to a stone house in Queenston, thought to be across from the Secords' and took Macdonell to Durham's farmhouse. He died the next day.

Portrait of Major General Sir Isaac Brock. Artist George Theodore Berthon.

It was only ten in the morning, but the Americans were convinced they'd won the battle. Up on the Heights, Captain Wool ordered his men to establish their position by building a fortification. Hundreds more American soldiers poured across the river, despite the heavy cannon fire from Vrooman's Point.

The British and Canadian troops had withdrawn to Durham's farm to await reinforcements from Fort George and from Chippawa, three miles above the falls. Brock had left word that Major General Roger Hale Sheaffe, the commander of Fort George, was to follow as soon as Brock had been able to determine where the enemy planned to make their full attack.

The counterattack began in the afternoon. Native warriors led by Lieutenant John Norton scaled the Heights from the southwest, taking the Americans — who were busy building their fortifications — by surprise.

Norton had been appointed chief by the Grand River Natives, and Isaac Brock had named him their commander. It had been Norton who cleverly devised the plan to ascend Queenston Heights at some distance along the road from Queenston, and to come at the Americans from behind. A brilliant tactician, he was respected by both Natives and whites for his superior education and his knowledge of the customs of both cultures.

Taunting the terrified Americans with their savage war whoops, the Natives skirmished with them, keeping them off-balance until the main force arrived under Major General Sheaffe.

Sheaffe, too, had planned a surprise attack. He'd reached Vrooman's about 11:00 a.m., but from there had taken a roundabout route through St. Davids and the farmland behind Queenston. Along with the troops that had arrived from Chippawa, he came up onto the Heights two miles west of the Americans.

The British had a force of nine hundred men, and with the militia, a company of black soldiers — the "Coloured Corps" from Niagara — and Norton's one hundred Natives, they advanced across the top of the Heights, pressing the Americans back toward the river. There was no place for them to go. Wool had been injured, and his successor, Colonel Winfield Scott, tried in vain to keep his men together.

Although a few Americans escaped down the hill to the village, others scrambled down the steep bank to the river, hoping to be picked up by one of their boats; still others panicked and went over the cliffs to their deaths.

Colonel Winfield Scott surrendered, and by 3:30 p.m. the Battle of Queenston Heights was over. Three hundred American soldiers and officers were captured. The next day, six hundred more were taken prisoner — men left stranded when their boats went home without them.

With Brock's victories at Michilimackinac and Detroit, and the American defeat at the Battle of Queenston Heights, the morale of the defenders of Canada grew immeasurably.

The death of Isaac Brock was a high price to pay for victory. The man who had been such an inspiration to his troops died before learning that he had been knighted for his victory at Detroit.

The body of Major General Sir Isaac Brock lay in state at Government House in Niagara. Both he and Lieutenant Colonel John Macdonell were buried with full military honours at Fort George on October 17, 1812, in a newly built bastion in the northeast corner of the fort. Macdonell, in rallying the men after Brock had fallen and leading the second attack on Queenston Heights in an attempt to recapture the redan, was also recognized as a hero.

The young Scottish-born Macdonell had been a lawyer at York and a politician. In 1811 he had assumed duty as the attorney general of Upper Canada. Brock had appointed him as provincial aide-de-camp in April 1812, with the rank of lieutenant colonel in the York Militia.

For the long funeral procession from Government House to the fort the road was lined with soldiers of every stripe, the militia, Native warriors, and thousands of civilians, who solemnly watched as the twin caissons carrying the caskets of Brock and Macdonell passed by. General Brock's trusted horse, Alfred, was also part of the procession, led along the road by four grooms, to the slow beat of the drums.

As Brock's body was laid to rest, the British gunners at Fort George fired a twenty-one-gun salute. The American guns across the river at Fort Niagara fired a matching salute, a mark of respect for the fallen hero.

5

A Seasonal War

The same thunderous roar of cannon fire that had roused Isaac Brock from his bed at Fort George before dawn on October 13 shook the ground at Queenston and reverberated through the Secord house. Laura bolted upright.

Before she'd opened the door to the children's room, thirteen-year-old Mary appeared in the hall. "I heard it, Mother. I'll help you get the little ones up."

Eleven-year-old Charlotte was already pulling clothes on over her nightshift. Harriet, who was nine, had her face pressed to the windowpane, trying to see what was causing the excitement. "It's another thunderstorm," she decided when the next flash of light illuminated the escarpment west of the house.

Laura lifted Appy from her bed. "Quickly; quickly!"

Charles had to be shaken awake. The three-year-old sat up, rubbing his eyes and scowling. "Don't want to," he complained, trying to shake off Mary, who was stuffing his chubby arms into his coat.

There was no time to grab more than a knitted coverlet. Laura, with two-year-old Appy on her hip, found Fan standing at the foot of the stairs, wringing her hands. She put an arm about her shoulders and herded the girl and the children out through the back door.

Bob had already gone ahead to set the farm animals loose, as James had instructed he should do in the event of an invasion.

"Pick-a-back." Mary crouched down to let the reluctant Charles clamber onto her back.

"Hurry; hurry!" They had to get to a safe place, away from the gunfire at Queenston. In the dim light of early morning the family made its way into the countryside.

"Cannon balls were flying around me in every direction," Laura recalled many years later. If only James were there. She had no way of knowing where his company of militia had taken him, and her worst fear was that he would be in the midst of whatever was happening.

About a mile from the village Laura and the children found shelter in a farmhouse where several other Queenston families had gathered. Although the children were safe for now, Laura was sick with worry over James. Throughout the whole day, while the children found ways to amuse themselves, the adults in the house listened to the sound of muskets and cannon. Every so often there would be a lull, and then the noise of gunfire would resume. *If only someone would bring some news!*

Finally, late in the afternoon, there was another lull. Would this one last? They waited. Even the children grew still. When only the occasional crack of a musket was heard in the distance, Laura could wait no longer. Leaving her children in the care of

Mary and the other women, she hurried back to Queenston.

The air was still thick with gun smoke when she entered her own property through the back, giving a rueful smile to find the cow patiently waiting for someone to open the gate, the pigs happily rooting in the weeds on the other side of their pen.

Before she reached the back door, a man wearing a bloodied bandage on his head came with the news that James had been wounded and was lying on the battlefield at Queenston Heights.

With a murmur of thanks, Laura pushed past the messenger. Her heart hammering in her throat, she lifted her skirts and climbed the steep hill to the scene of the battle, each step a prayer that James would not be badly hurt.

At the sight of the dead from both sides of the battle, and the moans of the injured and dying amongst them, Laura was filled with horror. She picked her way through all the red and blue uniformed figures on the ground until at last she found her husband.

James was weak from loss of blood and in great pain. In her haste to reach him, Laura had not thought to bring anything to staunch the flow of blood from his wounded shoulder. She tore a wide strip off the bottom of her petticoat and folded it to make a compress. Besides the shoulder injury, James had a musket ball lodged in his knee and could barely stand. A kind officer, whom Laura later referred to as "a Gentleman," came to her aid, and together they got James down off the hill and into his own house.

There, the Secords were in for another shock. The house had been ransacked, searched for valuables, and its contents turned upside down. During one of the lulls in fighting a few unscrupulous American soldiers had seized the opportunity to break into the deserted homes in the village and plunder them.

But this was not the time to grieve over their lost possessions. James was alive. Bob, who had returned by this time, helped Laura to make up a bed on the ground floor for him, and Laura bathed and dressed his wounds. By evening the children returned with the other villagers and were greatly relieved to find their father home.

Over the next few days the whole family prayed for James's recovery. A doctor from Fort George was finally able to attend him, but was unable to remove the shell from James's knee. He would never fully recover from this injury, and it would cause him pain for the rest of his life.

When James was a little stronger and could be moved, the family took him to St. Davids, where they planned to spend the winter. The house in Queenston would have to be repaired while they were gone.

Returning to St. Davids was a little like coming home. James had grown up in the tiny village, and he and Laura had spent the first few years of their marriage there among the members of his family. There were Secords on many of the farms in the area, and Laura would have plenty of help in caring for James. James's older brother, Stephen Secord, had died four years earlier, but Hannah and their seven children were still there, running the gristmill together.

While she was in St. Davids, Laura was relieved to learn that her half-brother Charles Ingersoll had survived the Battle of Queenston Heights. Charles had volunteered as a cavalryman in Thomas Merritt's Niagara Light Dragoons when the war first broke out. He was twenty-six. When the unit reorganized in 1813 as the Provincial Dragoons, under Merritt's son William Hamilton Merritt, Charles would be promoted to the rank of lieutenant. He would remain with the Dragoons until the end of the war. Charles Ingersoll would later marry William Merritt's sister Anna Maria and become a partner with Merritt in a mercantile business in St. Catharines.

James's brother, David Secord, who owned shops, mills, and businesses in St. Davids, had also fought at Queenston and survived. Unfortunately, his son, David Jr., had been taken prisoner by the Americans.

A favourite story of the Secord family, attributed to Laura's grandson James B. Secord, son of Charles Badeau, gives a different version of what happened after Laura found James on the battlefield that day.

Three enemy soldiers were standing over him, two with their muskets held as if they intended to club him to death. Laura flung herself over her husband's body, screaming that they should kill her and spare James. One of the men pushed her roughly aside, intent on his murderous deed.

Just in the nick of time, American captain John Wool stepped in and commanded the men to stop. Reprimanding them and calling them cowards, he had them taken to Lewiston under guard. Then he ordered a party of his own men to carry James down to his house. Wool didn't even make James a prisoner-on-parole, and reportedly often visited James after the war was over, the two becoming good friends.

A colourful story, but hardly true. James had been wounded in the afternoon battle when his Car Brigade saw action, and by the time Laura ascended the Heights, the British had taken back control of it. The Americans had surrendered.

As for Captain John Wool, he was back in Lewiston by this time, having his own wounds tended to.

—//—

In November 1812, American brigadier general Henry Dearborn, appointed senior major general in the American army after the resignation of Stephen van Rensselaer (brother of Solomon, who had landed at Queenston Heights), made two bungled attempts to invade Canada. Otherwise, most of the action in the war that winter took place farther to the east, on the St. Lawrence River and Lake Ontario.

Late in 1812, construction began on a fort at Prescott, a port on the St. Lawrence that seemed particularly vulnerable to an attack by the Americans, in a place where the river was narrow. Fort Wellington, which would be completed in 1814, was a one-storey blockhouse enclosed by earthen ramparts. Although it was not attacked, it did serve as a rallying place for British and Canadian troops crossing the river early in 1813 for the Battle of Ogdensburg.

After losing the Battle of Queenston Heights, the Americans returned to their side of the Niagara River, and the frontier remained quiet until the following spring.

The winter of 1812–13 was a hard one for the people of the Niagara area. Every merchant in Queenston had suffered consider-able losses during the battle, James Secord among them. His store had been vandalized and the shelves emptied of anything of value.

The people of the area shared what little they had with one another, and the Natives brought game to Queenston and St. Davids, providing the residents with a little meat. Even the British army was as generous with its stores as was possible.

—//—

Captain Isaac Chauncey of the U.S. navy had arrived in Sackets Harbor, New York, on the southeastern shore of Lake Ontario in October 1812. He would command the American naval effort on Lakes Ontario and Erie. In November his fleet of seven ships chased the British *Royal George* into Kingston Harbour. He was prevented from attacking the ship by the guns on shore, but he did manage to keep the British fleet bottled up at Kingston until winter came and the navigation season ended.

All through the winter both sides in the conflict continued constructing warships at a feverish pace, each side trying to out-build the other. British shipbuilders at Kingston and York were trying to match the American ship *Madison,* with its twenty-four guns. Across the lake at Sackets Harbor, Chauncey was building an even larger vessel.

During the first eight months of the war there had been a series of raids all along the St. Lawrence, and British supply boats on the river were constantly harassed. In September 1812, American troops stationed at Ogdensburg, New York, under Captain Forsyth of the 1st U.S. Rifles, raided Gananoque, Ontario. This resulted in a retaliatory attack by the British in October.

In February 1813, two hundred American soldiers and a number of volunteers crossed the ice at night to the Canadian side of the river and freed a group of American citizens held in the Brockville jail. Before fleeing back to Ogdensburg, they seized supplies, arms, and forty-five of the town's most promi-nent citizens. The Canadian captives were soon set free, but on February 22, eight hundred British troops and Canadian militia crossed the ice from Prescott and attacked Ogdensburg.

As a result of the Battle of Ogdensburg, a large part of the town was damaged, the fort dismantled, and the barracks burned. Captain Forsyth and some of his riflemen escaped overland to

Sackets Harbor, where he asked for additional troops to help him take back Ogdensburg. His request was denied.

As far as the people of Ogdensburg were concerned, Forsyth was responsible for the attack on their town. Under a flag of truce, British lieutenant colonel "Red George" Macdonnell, the commander of Fort Wellington at Prescott, had earlier come to see Captain Forsyth to complain about the continuous raids, but Macdonnell had been met with nothing but insults.

After the battle, the townspeople of Ogdensburg did not want any more American troops stationed there. None would return until October 1813. In the meantime, the citizens began selling food and supplies to the British troops across the river, a practice that would continue for the duration of the war.

In 1813, Sir James Lucas Yeo became the British Royal Navy's commander for Lake Ontario and Lake Erie. In the spring the fleets belonging to both Canada and the United States jockeyed up and down Lake Ontario, keeping an eye on each other but managing to avoid any major confrontations.

That all changed when, in April 1813, Chauncey's American fleet of fourteen ships led an invasion of York, sailing from Sackets Harbor to the western end of the lake. Under the command of Henry Dearborn, 1,700 American regulars disembarked before dawn at what is today Sunnyside Beach. Although York was the capital of Upper Canada, the garrison there was small, consisting of only about three hundred regulars, four hundred militia and dockworkers, and about fifty to one hundred Natives. The American troops easily drove back the small force that met them, while their warships demolished the batteries on the shore.

British general Roger Hale Sheaffe, who had become commander of forces and administrator of Upper Canada after Brock's death, advised the militia officers to surrender the town, to burn the naval storehouses, and to blow up the stone magazine in the small fort where the ammunition was stored, to keep it out of the enemy's hands. The explosion was so huge that it was heard as far away as Niagara. Tons of falling debris from the blast damaged property, and thirty-eight American soldiers were killed, another 222 wounded. Among the dead was American brigadier general Zebulon Pike, Dearborn's commander on shore.

Dearborn came ashore himself then to assume command, and the surrender was negotiated. Sheaffe and the British regulars abandoned the garrison at York, the militia was allowed to return home, and private property was ordered to be left untouched. But during their six-day occupation the Americans burned Government House — the residence of the lieutenant-governor — the parliament buildings, and other public buildings. When some of their shops and private homes were also robbed, the citizens of York felt they had been abandoned by the British.

In the invasion, the British lost their naval and military stores at York as well as a ship that had been under construction there. When the American fleet sailed away, it took with it one of the British vessels.

Now that York had been captured, the Americans set their sights on the Niagara frontier. The plan was that if attacks along the Niagara River turned out to be successful, the Americans would move on to Kingston.

The warmer weather had arrived, and James and Laura Secord and their five children left St. Davids and returned to their home in Queenston. It was time to prepare the ground for planting. Spring always brought new life, and the Secords were hopeful of a brighter future. But the war was not yet over, and in May it returned to the Niagara Peninsula.

On May 25, 1813, the American fleet under Commander Chauncey began a cannon bombardment of Fort George, setting its log buildings on fire. Because of the heavy shelling, Brigadier General John Vincent and his staff of regulars and militia were unable to stop the American troops under Colonel Winfield Scott, Dearborn's chief-of-staff, from landing two days later on the Canadian side.

After spiking the guns and destroying any ammunition they couldn't carry with them, Vincent hastily evacuated the fort, leaving behind the women and children who lived there. The British, outnumbered four to one, suffered heavy casualties: fifty dead and three hundred wounded or missing.

Vincent retreated with his troops along the Niagara River to Queenston, where he cut north, marching his men to a British supply depot in a farmhouse belonging to John De Cew (also De Cou) near Beaver Dams. The large, stone house had been built before the war by De Cew, and he'd offered it to the British army as a depot for supplies and ammunition. It occupied a commanding position, high on the escarpment.

The next day, Vincent sent the militia home and took the regulars to Burlington Heights (Hamilton) at the head of Lake Ontario, where there was an earthen fort. He ordered all the troops from the Niagara frontier to join him there — the troops escaping from Fort Erie, as well as those from Amherstburg on the western frontier. Burlington Heights gave the British a harbour-front location high above the lake and close by land routes to both York and Amherstburg.

Although the Americans were now in control of the whole of the Niagara Peninsula, they had not accomplished everything they had set out to do. They had planned to completely destroy Vincent's army, which would have left Upper Canada west of Kingston entirely in their hands.

While Chauncey's fleet had been busy softening up the defences at Fort George for the American attack, British commander Yeo had tried unsuccessfully to capture Sackets Harbor. When that failed, he sailed toward Burlington with troops and supplies for Vincent's army that had arrived there following the evacuation of Fort George.

In July 1813, Chauncey, in his new ship, the *General Pike*, with its twenty-six guns, would again head for York, where for the second time the American troops would occupy the town, seizing supplies and burning storehouses, although this time the damage would be less severe.

During the final weeks of navigation in 1813, Chauncey's fleet would control Lake Ontario. Regardless, small boats carrying British troops and Canadian militia between York and Kingston would still manage to get through unscathed. And in Kingston Harbour, the shipbuilders would continue to reinforce Yeo's fleet.

After Vincent had evacuated Fort George and retreated to Burlington Heights, the settlers in the Niagara region feared that the British were about to abandon them, believing that they were preparing to retreat to Kingston, leaving the western part of the province to the Americans. The Americans had taken Fort Erie, and when General Dearborn ordered a corps of American soldiers to pursue the British to Burlington Heights, they began to advance up the peninsula.

On June 5, a force of 3,400 American infantry made camp for the night in a field at Stoney Creek, where they would wait for the American cavalry to catch up before the attack on Burlington. They felt quite safe. They had the Niagara Escarpment on one side and a swamp on another. Their sentries were posted at the only place the encampment might be vulnerable.

They hadn't counted on a local boy named Billy Green, who'd been keeping an eye on the American troop movements, and who had told the British at Burlington Heights the location of the enemy camp.

Sometime after midnight on June 6, while the Americans slept, a force of 704 British soldiers led by commanding officer Lieutenant Colonel John Harvey advanced on the sentries who were guarding the encampment. Harvey had ordered his men not to use their muskets for fear of arousing the enemy; the element of surprise was crucial.

After silently bayoneting the American sentries, however, the British troops rushed the camp, cheering and waking up the Americans, who started shooting. What resulted was total confusion. In the dark, men fired on their own troops, and General Vincent, who'd been persuaded by Harvey to try the nighttime attack, got himself lost in the woods, not to be found until the next day by his men.

Before dawn, the fighting ended, but each side thought the other had won, and everyone left the scene. The Americans retreated as far as Forty Mile Creek (Grimsby), and the British went back to Burlington Heights, taking with them one hundred prisoners.

At Forty Mile Creek the Americans thought they would be safe, but on June 7 the British fleet suddenly appeared on the horizon. Farther inland, the dismissed Canadian militia and the Natives were beginning to assemble. The American general, Henry Dearborn, ordered all the American troops to retreat to

Fort George. His forces subsequently pulled out of Chippawa, and before leaving Fort Erie, set fire to it.

The Americans retreated from Forty Mile Creek so quickly that they left behind hundreds of tents, wagonloads of camping supplies, baggage, and barrels of flour. The British army picked up these supplies as they advanced. The people of Niagara would later delight in telling how it had taken the Americans four days to reach Stoney Creek, and less than one to run back.

Vincent moved all his troops from Burlington Heights, and within a few days he had detachments at Twenty Mile Creek (Jordan), Twelve Mile Creek (St. Catharines), De Cew's farm-house near Beaver Dams, and an advanced post near Ten Mile Creek. Reinforcements of British regulars arrived, and Vincent was able to send some on to Proctor at Amherstburg.

From their location at the western end of Lake Ontario, the British overlooked what was the no man's land of the Niagara Peninsula. For their part, the Americans remained in control of the area from Fort George, strategically located at the entrance to the Niagara River, and all the way to Queenston. But the Battle of Stoney Creek would be the last time the Americans would advance so deeply into the Niagara Peninsula. They retreated behind the damaged walls of Fort George and would only emerge for a few brief forays before winter set in.

6

The Green Tiger: Lieutenant James FitzGibbon

"Every man of serviceable military age should be considered and treated as a prisoner of war." That was the order issued by American general Henry Dearborn, and under the occupation of Queenston and area, over two hundred men were arrested and marched to an internment camp in Greenbush, near Albany, New York.

When Laura heard the stories of local men seized right from their beds or while working in the fields and taken to prison, it must have been a relief to her that James, though unable to return to the militia or to look after his store, was there with her and the children. The Americans had decided that James Secord, unable to walk more than two or three steps without assistance, and therefore posing no threat to them, would be permitted to remain at his home in Queenston.

To compensate for that concession, the Secords would be required to billet three American officers in their home. These men were to be given the two rooms upstairs as their living quarters and would eat their evening meals in Laura's dining room.

According to Harriet Secord Smith, James and Laura's third daughter, the behaviour of the American troops during the occupation of Queenston was nothing short of tyrannical. They would enter shops and private homes unannounced, looking for money and helping themselves to anything else they wanted. Aware that the citizens would have hidden whatever valuables they owned, the soldiers would even resort to shredding the family's bedding with bayonets or swords in their search.

Laura had managed to save her small collection of heirloom Spanish doubloons on one occasion, by tossing them into a kettle of hot water that hung on a crane over the flames of the kitchen fire.

Some sources tell the story of another time when three American soldiers entered the Secord house, intending to plunder its contents. Surprised at finding Laura there, one of the intruders told her that after the war was over he would be back and would claim all of the Secord property as his own.

Laura's angry retort was that the only piece of property in Queenston that man would ever own would be a six-foot grave. No one realized how prophetic her words were until, a few hours later, two of the men returned to tell her they had had an altercation with some Canadian soldiers earlier, and the third man had been killed.

If these renegades happened to be hungry, they thought nothing of stealing a family's provisions or raiding their vegetable garden. Although the Secord family with its five children had to put up with the inconvenience of being confined to the ground floor of their Queenston home, having the American officers take their evening meal at their house meant that the

American army regularly delivered a supply of food to Laura's door. At least her family would not starve.

Most of the burden of running the house and James's business now fell to her. She looked after his accounts and wrote letters to his customers and to those to whom he owed money. The children had their chores to do around the house — gathering eggs, feeding the livestock, and helping to keep ahead of the weeds in the vegetable patch — but most important was staying out of the way of the American officers. Fan helped out in the kitchen, while Bob tended to the heavier tasks.

There had been some criticism from the British military when Brigadier General John Vincent had not chased the Americans all the way back to Fort George from Stoney Creek and confronted the enemy there. One of those who voiced his objection to what he saw as Vincent's lack of offensive action was Lieutenant James FitzGibbon, in charge of a detachment of fifty hand-picked "Bloody Boys," who were based at De Cew's farmhouse. He believed that had Vincent followed up on the American retreat to Fort George, the fort could have been taken and the Americans driven back across the river.

James FitzGibbon had been born at Glin, in County Limerick, Ireland, in November 1780. He was the son of a weaver and farmer who owned a small piece of land on the Knight of Glin's estate. The boy left school at an early age and was just fifteen when he enlisted in a yeomanry corps, similar to Canada's militia, which supplied civilian defence at home. James was soon promoted to the rank of sergeant.

In 1798 he joined the Tarbert Infantry Fencibles and a year later was recruited into the 49th Regiment of the British Army.

He fought in campaigns against Napoleon in Holland and Denmark, where he served as a marine and earned the Naval General Service Medal.

The 49th Regiment was sent to Canada in 1802 and stationed at Quebec. Under the tutelage of Lieutenant Colonel Isaac Brock, the commander of the 49th, FitzGibbon rose through the ranks to become a lieutenant in 1809. Brock had seen the potential in the affable young man, and he became his unofficial mentor, encouraging him to better himself through private study and lending him books from his own library to read.

By the time war came to Canada, Lieutenant James FitzGibbon had been in the country ten years and was the commanding officer of a company. The ambitious young soldier had won the respect of his men, was well-liked and good-natured, and a natural leader — qualities he shared with his personal hero, Isaac Brock.

In 1812, FitzGibbon demonstrated skill and cunning when he successfully escorted a brigade of twenty-four small boats carrying supplies for the troops in Upper Canada from Montreal to Kingston, navigating the rapids in the St. Lawrence River without arousing the suspicion of the Americans on the opposite shore.

The next winter he conducted a brigade of forty-five horse-drawn sleighs carrying military stores, this time from Kingston to Niagara. It was a bitterly cold January when he led the trek of 250 miles around the shores of the Bay of Quinte and Lake Ontario, straight into a gale blowing snow off the lake.

In 1813, as the commanding officer of a company, FitzGibbon had participated in the Battle of Stoney Creek, but he'd been upset by the way the British officers had conducted themselves — rushing into the enemy camp cheering before they'd even formed themselves into a proper line of attack.

FitzGibbon had managed to persuade his commanding officer to let him form a special unit of men to be trained in a new style of warfare, one more suited to the ravines and wooded terrain that covered much of that part of Upper Canada. Once Brigadier General Vincent had approved the formation of the elite force, FitzGibbon went about selecting the men to serve under him. It seemed everyone in the 49th wanted to be on the team, but FitzGibbon selected only fifty from among the companies in the regiment.

These men were taught the tactics of guerrilla warfare, using surprise attacks, employing stealth and cunning, the same skills FitzGibbon had learned from the Natives. The group's main purpose, besides providing intelligence to the British Army and harassing the enemy, was to chase down and capture the renegade American raiding parties that had been terrorizing innocent civilians, particularly women and old men.

Worst among these groups was a small troop led by a doctor from Buffalo by the name of Cyrenius Chapin. Chapin's band would swoop down on Niagara farmers, capturing any ablebodied men among them, taking them prisoner and plundering their property.

As a doctor, Chapin had attended patients on both sides of the border before the war and was familiar with the roads through the Niagara region.

Chapin claimed he and his band were actually helping the settlers by protecting them from "merciless plunderers." Unless they happened to be American sympathizers, the locals did not appreciate Chapin's efforts, labelling him a scoundrel, and for many he was the most hated man on the Niagara frontier.

FitzGibbon divided his special team into three groups to facilitate their movement in the woods and so that the enemy would think there were more than only fifty. They used cowbells instead of bugle calls to signal one another, creating more noise and confusion for the opposition.

Because they wore grey-green jackets for camouflage, the men were called the "Irish Greens;" however, this team of fierce, fast-moving horseback riders quickly earned the name "Green Tigers." They preferred to call themselves the "Bloody Boys."

FitzGibbon planned to use his team in advance of the army. Always on the alert, the group never slept in the same place twice, and they could fight in the woods when necessary.

The Green Tigers' post at De Cew's farmhouse near Beaver Dams was surrounded by forest, ravines, and streams — the

Photograph of James FitzGibbon in later life wearing his Military Knight of Windsor uniform.

ideal terrain for the team to conduct its scouting and guerrilla drills. De Cew's was also strategically located near roads leading north to Twelve Mile Creek, northeast to Queenston, and southeast to Chippawa. The escarpment and creek would serve to slow down the approach of any invading force.

The tiny hamlet of Beaver Dams (Thorold) had gotten its name from a large population of beavers that inhabited the surrounding marshland. John De Cew was the community's most prominent citizen. A United Empire Loyalist from New Jersey, he owned mills and orchards and was connected to other business enterprises in the area. The large stone house he'd built before the War of 1812 had replaced the original log cabin he and his wife, Catherine Docksteder, had first lived in. Captain De Cew, who had commanded a company of the 2nd Lincoln County Militia, was one of the men who had been captured by American patrols and sent to prison in the United States. He would manage to escape in April 1814, and within a month would be back home.

Mrs. De Cew and her children continued to live in the upstairs rooms of the family home while FitzGibbon and his men used the lower level as their headquarters. It was a spacious house with large fireplaces, its walls lined with native black walnut. There was an orchard outside where De Cew had planted several different varieties of fruit trees, and his mills were used to grind grain for the British troops.

Chapin and FitzGibbon had been chasing each other for weeks, the Green Tigers always on the lookout for opportunities to force the American pickets back to the fort. After several clashes, Chapin decided he was going to put an end to it.

Intent on convincing the military authorities to attack the De Cew house, Chapin met with Lieutenant Colonel Charles Boerstler, a thirty-three-year-old from Maryland stationed at Fort George and a regular with the 14th U.S. Infantry. Chapin told Boerstler that he'd personally checked out the route to De Cew's house and found only one company there, plus fifty to a hundred Natives. He could lead Boerstler's army to De Cew's with five hundred men and a couple of field pieces, take the enemy, and wipe out the stronghold with no difficulty.

By June 16, FitzGibbon's elite team of fifty Green Tigers was at De Cew's. A party of Caughnawaga Natives, just recently arrived from Lower Canada under the command of Dominique Ducharme, was nearby.

Seven miles away, at the mouth of Twelve Mile Creek, Major Peter de Haren commanded two hundred men of the 104th Regiment. At Twenty Mile Creek, Colonel Cecil Bisshopp waited with a larger force, and General John Vincent with the main British force was back at Forty Mile Creek. Also on patrol in the area were William Merritt's volunteer horsemen, the Provincial Dragoons.

In total, the British and Canadians had only 1,600 men. If they had uniforms at all, they were in tatters; some men were even without shoes. But all were ready to face any invasion.

Lieutenant Colonel Boerstler, who considered Chapin "a vain and boastful liar" and possibly a disloyal one, was not impressed with the plan of attack the man laid out for him. He dismissed him, wishing him a curt "good-day."

Captain Chapin (he called himself "Major") went over Boerstler's head to Brigadier General John P. Boyd, General Dearborn's second-in-command, and the next thing Boerstler knew he was being ordered to lead five hundred men against De Cew's house, to capture the enemy and batter the place down.

It was a hurried operation, and Boerstler was told to leave immediately for Queenston with five hundred men and two guns. It was after 11:00 p.m. on the night of June 23. They were to stop in Queenston overnight and to go on to De Cew's early the next morning. By leaving the fort at night they'd avoid being seen by the inhabitants. Chapin would be the guide.

The mounted troops left Fort George, riding as quickly and as silently as possible to Queenston. There they ensured that all the citizens remaining in the occupied town were inside their homes where they would be prevented from sounding any alarm. Not even a candle was to be lit inside the houses.

The main body of the army would follow behind and join the cavalry at the encampment. No fires were to be allowed overnight, and the men would sleep on their guns. The success of the mission depended on catching the British by surprise. The last thing the Americans wanted was some resident slipping past the pickets they'd posted on the roads leading out of Queenston and alerting FitzGibbon as to what was about to happen.

Little did they know that, intent on doing exactly that, Laura Secord had already left.

7

The Walk to Beaver Dams

To this day, no one knows for sure exactly how, two days prior to the overnight encampment of the American troops at Queenston, Laura Secord found out about the plan to attack De Cew's farmhouse at Beaver Dams. She never revealed that part of the story.

"It was while the Americans had possession of the frontier, that I learned of the plans of the American commander," Laura said, rather vaguely, in a letter she wrote forty years after the Battle of Beaver Dams.

"Living on the Frontier during the whole of my life I had frequent opportunities of knowing the moves of the American forces," she explained in 1860, in a memorial she had prepared for the visiting Prince of Wales. "I was thus enabled to obtain important information which I deemed proper to communicate to the British commander Col. FitzGibbon, then Lt. FitzGibbon, of the 49th Regt."

Because there were American officers billeted in her home and taking their meals there, it is quite possible that Laura would sometimes overhear their conversation. On occasion, other American officers would turn up at mealtime, and Laura would have to see that they, too, were fed.

It may even have been her husband, James, who overheard a conversation between the officers. For fear of reprisal, both he and Laura kept the truth a secret for their entire lives.

We do know that Captain Chapin was in Queenston a few days before the Battle of Beaver Dams. The *Buffalo Gazette*, June 29, 1813, reported, "On Saturday week (19th June) the mounted men under Major Chapin passed down to Queenston."

Chapin's men had been involved in two altercations, and on the last, which the report states took place on June 21, one of his corps was captured by the enemy while he was asleep. It is also known that FitzGibbon's Green Tigers skirmished with Americans at Niagara Falls on June 20, and again on June 21 at Chippawa.

There is good reason to believe that Chapin, likely furious at losing another man to FitzGibbon, stopped off at the Secords' to talk to the officers there. He may have told them that he had a plan to deal with the dastardly FitzGibbon, and that he had convinced Brigadier General Boyd of the efficacy of his plan.

Chapin was a big man, over six feet tall, and boastful, according to Boerstler, with a voice that carried easily beyond the walls of the dining room. Chapin knew that the plan to capture FitzGibbon and destroy his outpost was being set in motion. FitzGibbon had to be gotten rid of before they could take on the British. Being the braggart he was, Chapin wouldn't pass up an opportunity to talk about it; the plan was his brainchild.

Laura had explained to Bob and Fan, the family servants, that she could not disobey the officers' requests to provide another place at the table. The servants were to put out all the food they had and were not to forget to include the liquor. While the men were eating and drinking, according to some stories, Laura is supposed to have slipped out of the house and overheard their conversation through an open window.

One source states that earlier one of the Americans had insulted Bob, and rather than have the man suffer any more abuse, Laura had waited on the table herself. If this was the case, the officers may simply have ignored her and continued their discussion as she went about clearing their plates and refilling their glasses.

Her granddaughter, Laura Secord Clarke, daughter of Laura Ann who was born to Laura and James three years after the War of 1812, gives this version of the conversation between her grandparents after they became privy to the American information, the way she remembered her grandmother telling it.

"James, somebody ought to tell Colonel FitzGibbon they are coming."

"Well, if I crawled there on my hands and knees, I could not get there in time," James replied.

"Suppose I go?" was Laura's suggestion. How could she not, knowing now what she did?

"You go, with a country in so disturbed a state? I do not think any man could get through, let alone a woman."

"You forget, James," said Laura, "that God will take care of me."

However it happened that the Secords learned of the enemy's plan of a surprise attack, or which one of them heard it first, they were in possession of a crucial piece of intelligence, and both agreed that FitzGibbon must be warned.

Like many people, Laura believed that FitzGibbon and the Indians were all that was stopping the Americans from pushing right on through the peninsula. And when that happened, it would be Loyalists like themselves who paid most heavily.

The first documentary evidence of Laura's walk was in a petition to Lieutenant-Governor Sir Peregrine Maitland, written by James Secord and dated February 25, 1820. James was requesting a licence to operate a stone quarry on a portion of a Queenston military reserve.

It reads, "The petition of James Secord, Senior, of the Village of Queenston, Esquire Captain in the 2nd Regiment of the Lincoln Militia, was wounded in the battle of Queenston, and twice plundered of all his moveable property … that his wife embraced an opportunity of rendering some service at the risk of her life, in going thro' the Enemies' Lines to communicate information to a Detachment of His Majesty's Troops at Beaver Dams in the month of June 1813 …"

Years later, in 1853, Laura herself wrote that once she knew of the Americans' plans she became determined to "put the British troops under FitzGibbon in possession of them, and if possible to save the British troops from capture or perhaps total destruction."

After the British had evacuated Fort George and gone to Burlington Heights, many inhabitants of Queenston had sent their families to the safety of homes of relatives living elsewhere. There really was no one else in the neighbourhood the Secords knew whom they could ask to relay the information now in their possession. There was no alternative; Laura would have to go.

Although deeply concerned for Laura's safety, James was well aware of how resolute the mother of his five children was. She was competent, too. The horror of the previous October and the Battle of Queenston Heights were never far from his mind. Laura had told him how she'd whisked the children off to a safe place, how she'd scoured the battlefield on Queenston Heights until she found him, and James would never forget how she'd gotten him down off the escarpment and home. Once she'd made up her mind to do something, there was no stopping her.

It was decided that Laura should leave early the next morning, June 22. In case the American attack was imminent, she had to get to De Cew's in time for FitzGibbon to mount a counterattack.

She would go first to St. Davids, three miles from Queenston. Her half-brother Charles Ingersoll was sick and was staying at Hannah Secord's house in the little village. Charles was engaged to Hannah's twenty-year-old daughter, Elizabeth, and the women in the house were doing what they could to nurse him back to health.

James suggested Laura might find her brother well enough to deliver the information to FitzGibbon himself. On the other hand, he pointed out, she might be able to persuade one of Hannah's sons to take over her mission.

There would have been little sleep for Laura that night. Convinced she was doing the right thing, she'd still be mulling over in her mind the safest route to take, well aware that if she were captured the penalty for spying was death by firing squad. She wouldn't let herself think about that.

Before dawn on June 22, she got up, and in the dark readied herself to leave the house, putting on the clothing she'd carefully chosen the previous evening: a brown cotton house dress that she'd made herself. The long straight skirt of the dress fell from a high waist, and with its elbow-length sleeves it would be cool enough. Over her shoulders she knotted a kerchief of light muslin, and slid her feet into her usual pair of low-heeled, kid leather slippers, tying them securely at the instep.

Before leaving the room she plucked a cotton sunbonnet off the peg to protect her fair complexion from the sun later in the day. For a moment Laura stood looking at her sleeping children, wishing she could say goodbye to them. But there'd been so much coming and going in the house since the occupation that it seemed as if even the walls had ears. She couldn't risk any noisy chatter at this hour. She tiptoed from the room without waking her brood and creaked open the door.

After the door had closed softly behind her, Harriet, who had turned ten that February, slipped out of bed and went to the window. She was the only one who saw Laura leave. It was about 4:30 a.m.

"I remember seeing my mother leave the house on that fateful morning," Harriet told author Sarah Anne Curzon in 1891, "but neither I nor my sisters knew on what errand she was bent."

Laura had assumed there would be American sentries posted ten miles out from Fort George, and for this reason she chose to take a roundabout route to St. Davids. It was her good fortune that the sentries were actually no farther out than two miles, and she never did run into them. Still, she had prepared an excuse for being on the road at dawn and would be confident in repeating it if she were stopped. She was going to visit her sick brother.

Charles was her favourite brother; the younger ones she barely knew. Thomas had been born just prior to the Ingersoll family's move from Queenston to the log house at Oxford-on-the-Thames, and Laura had remained behind to marry James. Two other half-brothers, Samuel and James, were born after Laura and her three sisters from her father's first wife were already married.

It had been Charles who'd told Laura everything she knew about Lieutenant James FitzGibbon. FitzGibbon's Green Tigers had much the same mandate as William Merritt's Provincial Dragoons in which Charles was a lieutenant.

At daybreak Laura arrived at St. Davids. The light breeze in which she'd first set off had disappeared, and already the air felt warm and humid. As soon as she reached Hannah Secord's house, down the lane and past the mill, she asked about Charles. The news was not good; he was still very sick and definitely not well enough to leave his bed.

Laura agreed to sit down for a short rest; she loved and trusted these people. She told her dear friend Hannah, Hannah's daughter Elizabeth, and Charles what she intended to do with the information she and James had unwittingly acquired. Charles may have been the one who suggested that Laura head farther north, take the long way around to Shipman's Corners (today's St. Catharines), rather than going directly to De Cew's. There was a good chance that if she went the way he suggested she might run into Captain William Merritt who lived at Twelve Mile Creek. He would be sure to help her. Certainly Merritt would leave immediately for Beaver Dams if she told him of the American plan to attack.

Hannah Secord's two oldest boys, who might have delivered the message to FitzGibbon had they been home, were both away with the militia. There was nothing anyone could say to dissuade her; Laura was determined to carry on. To her surprise, her niece Elizabeth offered to go with her. It might be safer to travel with a companion. But would the girl, who had never been very strong, be able to keep up?

Assuring Hannah and Charles that they would look out for each other, Laura and Elizabeth set out from St. Davids. By taking the roundabout route to Shipman's Corners they were less likely to encounter American sentries on the road. However, it greatly increased the distance they had to travel. It also meant having to follow the old trail through the dreaded Black Swamp with its many stories of mysterious disappearances.

The air between the dense cedars was filled with mosquitoes, and as they made their way toward the swamp, the ground under

Laura Secord on Her Journey to Warn the British. *Artist C.W. Jefferys, circa 1921.*

Courtesy of Archives of Ontario.

their feet became spongy. In the lowest areas, amidst the cattails, the black muck sucked at the light slippers the women wore, pulling them off their feet at every other step. They had to stop frequently, and Laura was growing concerned about Elizabeth. Laura herself, though small and appearing to be delicate, was wiry and strong, and she did not tire easily.

As the morning wore on, the temperature rose. By the time they reached Shipman's Corners it was obvious to Laura that Elizabeth was near exhaustion. She knew the girl must go no farther. Family records indicate that Elizabeth, never robust, died the following year. She and Charles Ingersoll were never to marry.

Fortunately, the Secord family had friends at Shipman's Corners, and Laura left her niece in their capable hands to continue on her journey alone.

On blistered feet, Laura turned south, heading toward De Cew's, wishing she could be certain that by this time she was in British-held territory. By avoiding the road and any American sentries, she now ran the risk of encountering wild animals. She tried not to think about the wolves and wildcats that prowled the area, nor the masses of rattlesnakes that might be hiding from the blistering sun amongst the rocks.

She crossed fields of long grass and thistles that plucked at her skirts before she reached the woods. She didn't believe half the stories she'd heard about atrocities committed by the Indians, but she knew there were hundreds of them camped in these woods. Although she knew that the Natives in these parts were friends of the British, she was a woman out here on her own. She pushed her sunbonnet off her damp forehead and carried on.

Laura was using Twelve Mile Creek as a guide, never going far from it for fear of getting lost. If Hannah had provided her with some food for the journey it would be gone long before this. At least the water of the creek would quench her thirst and cool her hands and face.

It had been an unusually rainy spring, and the creeks and streams had flooded their banks. In one place, where Laura had been expecting to cross the creek, she discovered that the footbridge had been swept away.

She followed the creek bank, breaking through the brush and tangle of willows, coming upon a spot where a tree had fallen across the water. Pulling up her skirts, she dropped down and crawled across it on hands and knees until she reached the other side. The bank was slimy with mud, and she had to grasp at any protruding roots she could. Her feet sliding from under her, she hung on and managed to pull herself to the top.

About seven o'clock that evening she reached a steep, wooded embankment and began the ascent, feeling the fatigue in the muscles of her legs. Both her slippers were gone by this time, her dress muddied and torn, her face and arms scratched by brambles. She stumbled on, thinking she should soon see the lights of De Cew's farmhouse, and what a welcome sight that was going to be.

Suddenly, pushing her way through the last of the under-brush, Laura found herself at the edge of a clearing. She was surrounded by Native warriors.

The scene in the moonlight was terrifying. When they saw her, the Indians "all arose and with some yells, said 'Woman,' which made me tremble. I cannot express the awful feeling it gave me," Laura said later, "but I did not lose my presence of mind. I was determined to persevere."

She reminded herself that Native warriors had fought and died with the British in the American War of Independence, and with that thought she managed to keep her composure.

"I went up to one of the chiefs, made him understand that I had great news for Capt. FitzGibbon and that he must let me pass to his camp, or that he and his party would all be taken. The chief at first objected to let me pass, but finally consented, after some hesitation, to go with me and accompany me to FitzGibbon's station."

The Indians, most likely some of Dominique Ducharme's Caughnawaga, who had recently arrived in the area, helped Laura to walk the last mile in the dark, through De Cew's field to the farmhouse on the old Mountain Road from St. Davids.

She had walked for seventeen hours and covered nineteen miles (thirty kilometres), and although she would not be able to tell FitzGibbon how the American attack would occur, nor when, she was confident that he provided the best chance for the British to hold on to Niagara.

Lieutenant FitzGibbon must have been surprised when a strange woman appeared at the door of his outpost, dirty, barefoot, and obviously exhausted. As Laura wrote later, "I had an interview with him. I told him what I had come for and what I had heard — that the Americans intended to make an attack upon the troops under his command and would, from their superior numbers, capture them all." Then she dropped onto a chair, and one of FitzGibbon's men hurried to fetch her some water to drink.

FitzGibbon questioned Laura until he was convinced that she was not a spy. After all, she had come from Queenston, which was in the hands of the Americans.

After receiving Laura's information, FitzGibbon alerted the Natives, and together with his own men they took up positions all night from which they could intercept any attack.

But first, because Laura was worn out, FitzGibbon had one of his men take her to the Turney farm, far enough away that she would be safe and could get some rest. Mrs. Turney gathered her up like a mother hen, filling a basin with water so that she could wash her hands and face, and finally setting her blistered feet into it. After making sure Laura had eaten, she insisted on putting her to bed.

Years later, FitzGibbon wrote, "Mrs. Secord was a person of slight and delicate frame and made this effort in weather excessively warm, and I dreaded at the time that she must suffer in health and consequence of fatigue and anxiety, she having been exposed to danger from the enemy, through whose line of communication she had to pass."

It had been Laura's opinion, when she set out that day, that the attack would come the following morning, June 23. But nothing happened right away. The American troops were still back at Fort George, waiting until late evening to leave. They would stop that night at Queenston.

Source: Collections Canada.

Laura Secord Delivers Her Message to Lieutenant James FitzGibbon at De Cew's. *Artist C.W. Jefferys.*

Very early on the morning of June 24, one of Dominique Ducharme's Indian scouts raced up to FitzGibbon's headquarters to say they had encountered Colonel Boerstler's advanced guard on the road between Queenston and St. Davids, and one of the scouts had been killed.

Laura's intelligence had been correct. The American army was on its way.

8

Ambush in the Beech Woods: The Battle of Beaver Dams

Although no American troops had appeared on June 23, FitzGibbon did not sit idly by, waiting for something to happen. He sent word of the imminent attack to Lieutenant Colonel Bisshopp at Twenty Mile Creek and to Major Peter de Haren stationed near Shipman's Corners at Twelve Mile Creek. De Haren's position happened to be several miles from the place where Laura Secord had earlier crossed the creek.

FitzGibbon asked that he be sent reinforcements as soon as possible, although he knew they were not likely to reach him in time. His best hope lay with the Natives, four hundred of whom had gathered within two miles of his headquarters at De Cew's. Forty-eight-year-old militia captain Dominique Ducharme, a former fur trader, was in charge of 180 Caughnawaga and other Natives from Lower Canada. Ducharme's commanding officer was Colonel De Haren.

Captain William Johnson Kerr, twenty-six-year-old son-in-law of the late Chief Joseph Brant, who had led part of the Six Nations to the Grand River following the American War of Independence, had assembled two hundred warriors from among the Six Nations at Brantford, along with seventy or eighty Natives from various other tribes in Upper Canada. Kerr had fought at Queenston Heights alongside his cousin, John Brant, son of Joseph, as well as with John Norton.

The Natives had not been content to sit and wait either. On June 23, Ducharme and twenty-five of his warriors went on a scouting expedition. Although they had not seen any troops advancing, they had spotted a barge filled with American soldiers on the Niagara River, near Fort George. The Natives had fired on the vessel, killing four and taking seven prisoners. They'd been chased by the American cavalry, and one of two escaping warriors, who'd been left behind to capture horses, had been made a prisoner. The rest had all managed to slip away into the woods and disappear.

Very early on the morning of June 24, word came from another of the Native scouts that the Americans were advancing along the mountain road. Ducharme had previously reconnoitred the area in the vicinity of Beaver Dams and had chosen what he considered the best place for an ambush — a ravine in a thick forest of beech trees, where the heavy canopy of leaves kept out the sun. Here the road narrowed, becoming not much more than a wheel track.

Ducharme's men, like FitzGibbon's Green Tigers, were well-trained for fighting in the woods. Twenty-five Caughnawaga were placed in the trees on the right side of the road with Ducharme's lieutenants DeLorimier and LeClair. The Mohawk, under Captain Kerr, were stationed on the left. The rest of the warriors, led by

Ducharme himself, were put on a bank farther along, in a position where they could force the enemy back into the ravine.

Lieutenant James FitzGibbon rode up to a high point where he would be hidden from view and yet able to observe the approach. Shortly after 9:00 a.m. the long column of American soldiers appeared.

Captain Cyrenius Chapin rode in front with the grey-uniformed, mounted militia. Next came Colonel Charles Boerstler with three hundred of the 14th Infantry Regiment — the foot soldiers in their blue jackets, white trousers, and cockaded hats. These were followed by the artillery under the command of Captain Andrew McDowell, with two wagons drawn by four-horse teams and loaded with ammunition. Other wagons, or limbers, pulled the field guns — a 6- and a 12-pound gun. One hundred soldiers of the 6th and 23rd Regiments came next, led by Major Taylor, and twenty cavalrymen rode in the rear.

Those men near the front of the column could see the open field ahead that was their destination, the place where they would do battle in open lines, as they had been trained. They had tramped all the way from Queenston in the long column and were tired and thirsty, but at last the end was in sight. Because of their encounter with the Native scouts on the road that morning, Colonel Boerstler knew that their approach was no longer a surprise.

Suddenly, the air was filled with savage war cries. The Natives opened fire. Shots rang out from the trees on either side of the ravine, and several of the American cavalry in the rearguard were killed. The Natives crossed the road behind the troops, cutting off any retreat.

Up near the front of the column, Colonel Boerstler was wounded in the thigh, and Major Taylor's horse fell from under him. In desperation, Boerstler ordered his wagons and horses moved some distance away, out of reach of the Natives' fire. Unaccountably, Captain Chapin seemed to have vanished. He was later discovered with his men, taking shelter by the ammunitions wagons.

Hiding the fact that he had been wounded, Boerstler ordered Chapin's men to regroup, and he led them in a charge against the Natives. Trapped as they were in the narrow road, caught in the crossfire with no way to move forward or back, the charge was futile. Except for firing at random into the woods, there wasn't much the Americans could do. The forest was veiled in gun smoke, and the enemy concealed in the trees was decimating Boerstler's troops.

There was no way out for the Americans, but still the battle had raged for nearly three hours when Boerstler realized they were running out of ammunition. He kept trying to rally, although it was impossible to fight an enemy that never showed itself. So many of his men had been wounded that he detached a man from each unit to load the injured onto wagons and move them out of the way, into a more protected position.

If only he could force the enemy into the open fields beyond the beech woods. He was well aware that there were no American reinforcements coming for him. He was equally aware that the British had regular troops stationed in the area, and that if they hadn't already arrived, they would shortly be on the scene.

When FitzGibbon saw that the Americans were starting to panic, and because he wanted to avoid any further bloodshed, he had a bugler sound a ceasefire. With some of his Green Tigers he rode up to the American line, waving a white handkerchief tied to his sword.

From the outset, Colonel Charles Boerstler had not been having a good day. Captain Chapin had proved not to be the guide he'd boasted he was. By the time they'd reached St. Davids that morning it was obvious that the former doctor was confused about which road to take. Boerstler had had no choice but to stop and ask for directions. In the end, he took one of the locals along to act as their guide. It was later proved that Chapin had never before been within several miles of Beaver Dams.

Like the day Laura Secord had made her walk, the weather was hot and humid. Boerstler's men were tired after the long march over hills and down into valleys in the blazing sun. They had not stopped to rest, and they hadn't eaten since leaving Queenston. And now Boerstler was asking himself if Captain Chapin had deliberately led them into a trap.

Lieutenant FitzGibbon offered to negotiate, and Colonel Boerstler sent his artillery captain, Andrew McDowell, to talk with him. Then FitzGibbon began his elaborate bluff, telling McDowell that Major De Haren had sent him to demand the Americans surrender at once.

FitzGibbon had to delay as long as possible, had to keep the Americans talking in hopes that the reinforcements would arrive in the meantime. He told McDowell that the Americans were greatly outnumbered because the British reinforcements had arrived. Not only that, he said, but he'd received a fresh lot of Natives from the northwest, warriors who'd be much harder to control than the ones the Americans had been fighting all morning. To avoid a possible massacre, it would be in their best interest to surrender.

Captain McDowell returned to his commanding officer and made his report. At first Colonel Boerstler refused; he was not about to surrender to an enemy he'd never even seen.

McDowell went back to FitzGibbon.

"Perhaps," FitzGibbon suggested, "the officer would like to examine the British force to prove the Americans are indeed outnumbered?" It was a bold move, considering all he had were his Green Tigers.

With one out of five of his troops dead, Boerstler agreed to surrender, but first he must be allowed to see the size of the British force. FitzGibbon's bluff had been called.

Just at the right moment, Captain John Hall rode up with a dozen Provincial Dragoons and a few militiamen. The three Kelly brothers, who'd been allowed to return to their fields to help get in the hay, had heard the sound of gunfire and, seizing their muskets, had hurried toward the beech woods. Along the way more militiamen had joined them.

Captain Hall became part of the ruse when FitzGibbon convinced him to impersonate De Haren. He sent word back to Colonel Boerstler that "Colonel De Haren" would receive one of the American officers.

This time, Boerstler sent a lower-ranking officer, who readily accepted Hall as De Haren. Still stalling for time, Hall played along and refused to allow his troops to be inspected, pretending to be insulted by the request, and insisting he had a large enough force that the Americans should surrender.

Boerstler asked to be given more time, but FitzGibbon warned him that all the time he could give him before he lost control of the Natives was five minutes. It was FitzGibbon's hope that the surrender would be finalized before the real De Haren, his superior officer, showed up. All the while, he kept his Green Tigers moving back and forth, joining the Native forces on either side of the road, making it appear there were twice as many men as there were.

With no possibility of a seventeen-mile retreat to Fort George, with his men in their state of exhaustion and at the mercy of the

Indians, Boerstler surrendered. He sent Captain McDowell back to get the best terms he could.

The American officers would become prisoners of war, and the militia would return home to the United States, on parole. There was to be no looting; the private property of the American troops was to be respected. But now FitzGibbon was wondering how to disarm the Americans without them discovering that he'd been bluffing.

Another stroke of luck: Major De Haren with two hundred men of the 8th and 104th Regiments galloped up just in time to sign the capitulation papers.

FitzGibbon, speaking in a low tone, reminded De Haren that the men were already his prisoners. "Shall I proceed to disarm the American troops?" he asked, stepping away from De Haren's mount.

"You may," replied the colonel, and he ordered the Americans to march though the British ranks and lay down their arms on the other side. FitzGibbon recognized the danger in this. If the Americans were to walk through and put their arms down on the other side, they would surely discover just how few British there were.

Thinking quickly, FitzGibbon suggested, in a voice loud enough to be heard by the enemy, that the Natives might react badly at seeing the captured Americans still with their arms.

Just as FitzGibbon had hoped he would, the nervous Boerstler demanded his men be allowed to give up their arms at once, right where they stood, and begged only that the Natives be kept away from them.

FitzGibbon had not lost a single one of his men during the Battle of Beaver Dams. They had only come in at the end of the attack anyway, in order to fool the Americans into thinking hundreds of reinforcements had arrived. Dominique Ducharme lost fifteen Natives and twenty-five were wounded. The Americans had thirty fatalities and twice that number had been wounded. Four hundred and sixty-two American soldiers, including twenty-two officers, their two field guns and wagons, surrendered to FitzGibbon and his fifty Green Tigers.

In the memorial to the Prince of Wales, written for his visit to Canada in 1860, Laura Secord wrote the following about her ordeal: "I returned home next day, exhausted and fatigued … and when I look back I wonder how I could have gone through so much fatigue, with the fortitude to accomplish it."

When the sounds of the battle had faded away, Laura returned to her home in Queenston. One source states that a British officer accompanied her for a certain distance, possibly to a point where there would be no danger of her catching up with the dispirited American troops who were making their way back to Fort George.

9

Aftermath

Bless their hearts, her dear children, and James resting there in the sunshine on the bench beside the door, his stick across his knees. Laura didn't want to think how close she had come to never seeing them all again.

Her middle child, Harriet, was absorbed in watching Bob paint the white stones that lined the walk. Laura had promised herself that when this war was finally over she'd plant roses there instead.

Four-year-old Charles was chasing the hens across the yard, sending them squawking into the bushes, much to the amusement of little Appy, who clapped her hands in delight.

"Mama! You're back!" Harriet was the first to see her and jump to her feet.

Charles and Appy came running, and, crouching down, Laura received them both into her arms. They were hot and damp and smelled of the grass.

"I *told* Charles not to chase the hens," Harriet said. "You tell him, Mother. Tell him he'll frighten them so's they won't lay any more eggs."

The door of the house flew open then and Mary hurried out wearing her muslin cap, a dust cloth in her hand. "Mother," she cried. "At last, you're home!"

"They've gone, Mama." Harriet danced in front of her. "The officers. They've gone. Papa says we can move our things back upstairs. Isn't it wonderful?"

"Wonderful indeed," said James. His eyes fixed on Laura's face, he got slowly to his feet. "Come inside, my dear. Tell me how you found your brother. Has his health improved?"

Mary ushered her parents inside. "I'll make us some tea. Charlotte's gone with Fan to look for strawberries." She hesitated a moment, frowning. "Whose shoes are you wearing, Mother? And did you know you've torn your dress somehow? Look, right here. Oh, and here, too."

"A cup of chocolate for me, please," said Charles, and he slid his stout legs along the bench at the kitchen table. "You sit right here, Mama. I missed you very much."

In his official report to Colonel Cecil Bisshopp, Lieutenant James FitzGibbon gave credit for the victory over the Americans at Beaver Dams to the Natives. "In this affair the Indian warriors under the command of Captain Kerr were the only force actually engaged, to them the merit is due, and to them I feel particularly obliged for their gallant conduct on this occasion."

Unfortunately, this report was never seen by the Natives. FitzGibbon was the one who was heralded as the hero of the battle, given all the credit by the newspapers and the general public.

The *Montreal Gazette*, July 6, 1813, reported, "We have much satisfaction in communicating to the public the particulars of a campaign not of a *General* with his *thousands* but of a *lieutenant* with his *tens* only. The manner in which a bloodless victory was obtained by a force so comparatively and almost incredibly small with that of the enemy, the cool determination and the hardy presence of mind evinced by this highly meritorious officer ... with his little band of heroes, and the brilliant result ... (will) make known to the world the name of Lieutenant FitzGibbon ... and class the event with the most extraordinary occurrences of the present accursed war."

As previously mentioned, under the terms of the surrender at the Battle of Beaver Dams there was to be no looting of private property. However, looting was standard practice in warfare in those days. When the British had evacuated Fort George in early June and moved to Burlington Heights before the Battle of Stoney Creek, the invading American forces had taken the weapons from the dead British officers and had stripped the clothing off their bodies.

Considering it a reward for their part in the Battle of Beaver Dams, the Mohawk took swords, guns, and jackets from the Americans, but they did not do any harm to the bodies. Captain Dominique Ducharme had given his word to FitzGibbon that this would not happen.

The Natives were not the only ones looting. One source states that a British officer helped himself to some of the booty, seizing a pistol, a splendid black horse, and its saddle and bridle.

With virtually no help from the British, the Indians had forced the Americans to surrender at Beaver Dams, prompting Mohawk Chief John Norton's famous, wry comment, "The

Caughnawagan Indians fought the battle, the Mohawks of the Six Nations got the plunder and FitzGibbon got the credit."

Following the surrender, all the American forces along the Niagara frontier drew back to Fort George and Newark for the rest of the summer. The war wasn't over yet, but no longer did the Americans, whose morale had sunk to a new low, think it was going to be an easy victory. Twice in one month they'd suffered defeat at the hands of a much smaller force. The buildup of the Native troops following the battle worried the Americans, and they became fearful of them as they had been of old.

After the American loss at Beaver Dams, President James Madison demanded the resignation of General Dearborn, who had commanded the American army on the frontier from Niagara to the Atlantic coast. His replacement was Major General John Wilkinson. Although Colonel Charles Boerstler, too, was criticized for the fiasco, an American Court of Inquiry later blamed the American loss on volunteers like Cyrenius Chapin.

Chapin had been taken prisoner by the British at Beaver Dams and held at Burlington Heights. On July 12, he and twenty-eight of his men were being transported in two boats to Kingston for further incarceration. Early in the voyage, Chapin signalled to the men in the other boat to come alongside the one he was travelling in and to board it. A struggle ensued and Chapin's men overpowered the guards. They turned the boats around and arrived at Fort George the next day, free men. At the end of December, Chapin would again be taken prisoner when the British burned Buffalo. This time he would be escorted under heavy guard to a jail in Quebec.

The whole Niagara Peninsula breathed a sigh of relief when the enemy was driven back to Fort George. Those Canadian volunteers who could be spared for a few days were allowed to return to their homes to try to gather what they could of the year's crops, but there were few enough of them to accomplish the task, and much of the harvest was left to rot.

Laura Secord returned to her home in Queenston and picked up the pieces of her life, caring for James and the children, managing the household. No word was ever spoken about her brave deed, except perhaps privately between James and herself. No doubt he told her of his anxiety after she'd left that morning and of how his fears had increased when the large force of Americans had camped overnight in the village, prior to the attack at Beaver Dams.

Although the Americans had ended their occupation of Queenston, considering the uncertainty of war it would not have been wise to talk publicly about Laura's exploit. There were others, too, who had been involved in the mission: Hannah and Elizabeth Secord, Laura's half-brother Charles, and the Turneys, who had taken her into their home following her ordeal, and had fed her and put her to bed. If the story were ever to leak out, these people, too, could be subject to reprisals, and wisely, everyone kept silent on the subject.

Eight years after the Battle of Beaver Dams, Captain William Johnson Kerr, who'd tried in vain to get recognition for the important part the Natives had played in the battle, addressed a memorial to the Duke of York. In requesting a pension for himself, Kerr outlined the part he and the Natives had played in the battle.

Colonel James FitzGibbon also prepared a testimonial to accompany Kerr's petition. It stated, "Not a shot was fired from our side by any but the Indians. They beat the American detachment into a state of terror, and the only share I claim is the taking advantage of a favourable moment to offer them protection from the Tomahawk and the scalping knife. The Indian Department did all the rest."

FitzGibbon's skill and cunning, as well as his humanity, were instrumental in making the victory at Beaver Dams a major one. He stayed with his Green Tigers until October 1813, when he was made captain in the Glengarry Light Infantry, or Fencibles, one of only two regular army units raised in Canada. For FitzGibbon it was a long-sought-after promotion.

Captain FitzGibbon would go on to see further action in other battles in the War of 1812, joining the British raid on the American supply depot at Black Rock in July 1813, an attempt to steal salt that was needed to cure meat and to steal uniforms for the soldiers, many of whom were in rags and without shoes. His commander, Lieutenant Colonel Cecil Bisshopp, was mortally wounded in the raid. FitzGibbon was also in on the lengthy siege at Fort Erie the following summer.

Early in August 1814, based on his excellent record, FitzGibbon was permitted a short leave of absence in order to get married. Wanting to ensure that his sweetheart, Mary Haley, would receive an army officer's pension if he were to be killed in action, he sent her a message to meet him in Adolphustown, a Loyalist village west of Kingston. He went by boat as far as the Carrying Place and then rode horseback sixty miles, got married, and left his bride there on the church steps, returning immediately to the war.

He did survive, and he and Mary lived in Canada for many years, raising four sons and a daughter. When his regiment was disbanded and he was forced to go on half-pay, FitzGibbon began a career in public service in 1816. He became assistant adjutant general of Upper Canada in 1822, and in 1826 became a colonel in the York Militia. Colonel FitzGibbon also took part in suppressing the Rebellion of 1837, retiring from government service in 1842.

After the death of his wife, FitzGibbon spent some time in Belleville at the home of his eldest son, William. William had married Agnes Moodie, the daughter of Susanna Strickland Moodie, who was the author of the Canadian classics *Roughing It in the Bush* (1852) and *Life in the Clearings Versus the Bush* (1853).

Later, FitzGibbon went to England, where he was made a military knight at Windsor Castle for his services to the Crown. Though he often longed to return to Canada, he was never able to afford to do so. Colonel James FitzGibbon died at Windsor Castle on December 12, 1863, and was buried in the crypt of St. George's Chapel. He was eighty-three.

Laura Secord's name was never mentioned in the official reports of the Battle of Beaver Dams. It would be years before the part she played in it was made known. FitzGibbon left her out of his accounts, probably because any publicity about her deed could have been dangerous for her and her family. Although it might appear that he had slighted her with this omission, he did later prove himself to be a good friend.

In a certificate dated February 26, 1820, Captain James FitzGibbon, in support of James Secord's previously mentioned petition for a licence to operate a stone quarry on military land near Queenston, wrote:

> I certify that Mrs. Secord, Wife of James Secord of Queenston, Esquire, did in the Month of June, 1813, come to the Beaver Dam and communicate to me information of an intended attack to be made by the Enemy upon the Detachment then under my command there, which occasionally occupied a large Stone House at the place. The information was substantially correct, and

a detachment did march for the Beaver Dam, (on the morning of the second day after the information was given) under the command of Lieut. Colonel Boerstler, which detachment was captured. Mrs. Secord arrived at my station about sunset of an excessively warm day, after having walked twelve miles, which I at the time thought was an exertion which a person of her slender frame and delicate appearance was unequal to make.

"James Fitzgibbon"
Captn. Half Pay
York 26th February, 1820
"Late Gleng'y Lt. Infantry"

10

The Death of Tecumseh

As long as the British navy maintained a presence on Lake Ontario, the vital line of communication between Kingston and York was kept open and troops and supplies were able to reach Upper Canada. Neither the British nor the Americans seemed to know which side had control of the lake. The two fleets sailed around each other, entering into only minor dust-ups, and running for cover to Kingston or Sackets Harbor whenever necessary.

It was a different story on Lake Erie.

On August 5, 1813, Commodore Oliver Perry, who commanded the American fleet on Lake Erie, got the last of his ships out over the sandbar that protected the entrance to the American harbour at Presque Isle (Erie, Pennsylvania) and sailed into Lake Erie. He was ready to force the commander of the British naval squadron, Robert Barclay, to come out of his harbour at Amherstburg and face the American fleet.

For his part, Barclay knew he had to try to rid Lake Erie of the menace of the American ships, especially in light of the situation at Fort Amherstburg, where Lieutenant Colonel Henry Proctor's 1,400 followers, many of them Native warriors and their families, were on the verge of starvation.

Proctor had been put in command of Amherstburg by Major General Isaac Brock after the capture of Detroit. But with the Americans now poised to take control of Lake Erie, the British knew they weren't going to be able to hang onto the territory that comprised most of Michigan, the area that forces under Brock and his Shawnee ally, Tecumseh, had captured back on August 16, 1812.

Ever since the spring attack on York, Barclay had been short on cannon, and in order to equip his newest ship, *Detroit*, he had had to resort to a collection of cannon of various size and range, borrowed from Fort Amherstburg.

Of the six warships under Barclay's command, only three were adequately armed. He was going to have to go into battle against Perry's ten ships, which were all well-outfitted with proper naval guns. To make matters worse, the crews on Barclay's ships were surviving on only half rations.

The Battle of Lake Erie took place on September 10, 1813. It was all over by late that afternoon. The British fleet was defeated, although both sides had suffered terrible losses. Barclay and all the other British survivors were taken prisoner. The gallant Perry made sure his officers treated the prisoners with compassion, and he urged the government in Washington to grant Barclay, who had been badly injured, an immediate and unconditional parole. Barclay later referred to Oliver Perry as "a valiant and generous enemy."

With the Americans now in control of the lake, Proctor knew Detroit would have to be evacuated and that Fort

Amherstburg was in danger. He had lost one-third of his troops in the battle on the lake, and the cannon from his fort had gone to arm Barclay's new ship. Whatever supplies and provisions Major General Vincent might be able to send would now have to come overland.

It seemed to Proctor that the best thing for him to do was retreat up the valley of the Thames River toward Vincent's army. He would set up a defensive position farther along, where his men could take on the Americans, led by Brigadier General William Henry Harrison. The Natives, under the leadership of the Shawnee chief, Tecumseh, wanted to remain at Amherstburg and fight.

Tecumseh had a deep-seated hatred of the American commander, Harrison. Once the governor of Indiana, Harrison had destroyed Prophetstown, the capital of Tecumseh's confederacy, in the Battle of Tippecanoe, in 1811 in western Indiana.

Tecumseh and his brother, Tenskwatawa, also known as the Prophet, had tried to organize a confederacy of the Indian tribes that were being threatened by the continuing westward advance of American settlement. They felt that if the tribes were united they'd be strong enough to resist the pressure of the American government. But there was no room for the Natives in Harrison's expansionist plans.

Tecumseh had been away, looking for support for his confederacy from the Natives in the south, when Harrison marched an army into Indian territory on the Tippecanoe River. On November 7, 1811, the Prophet attacked the advancing American force. After a fierce battle, the Indians were defeated, and the Americans destroyed the town and all its food supplies.

Now at Fort Amherstburg, Tecumseh was urging Proctor to stay and face the enemy at the water's edge. But Proctor thought that if he retreated into Upper Canada along the Thames he could stretch Harrison's line of supply, giving the British time to fortify a defensive position.

Francis de Rottenburg, the replacement for General Roger Hale Sheaffe as commander of the forces in Upper Canada, was of the opinion that Perry's American ships would be laid up for a while after the Battle of Lake Erie. He thought Proctor should use the time available to him to try to appease the Natives.

Somehow Proctor was able to get Tecumseh's grudging agreement to his plan. On September 23 the British burned and abandoned Fort Amherstburg and Proctor's army headed toward Sandwich (Windsor). Tecumseh's mood was not optimistic. "We are going to follow the British," he said to his people, "and I feel that I shall never return."

Over at Detroit, the British force stationed there destroyed the barracks and public buildings and moved the army's rearguard across the river. The Americans weren't far behind.

Perry's ships transported Harrison and his troops to a landing at Fort Amherstburg. More reinforcements had arrived, and the American force setting out after Proctor was now 3,500 strong.

By October 5, the enemy was practically on Proctor's heels. He had no choice but to turn and make a stand. Less than five hundred of his men were fit to fight; the rest were either sick with fever or worn out from the battle on the lake. Tecumseh's Native force numbered about eight hundred.

Near Moraviantown, on the Thames River, Proctor's two thin lines turned and faced the enemy in a short, bloody battle. Although Proctor kept trying to rally his men, urging them not to give up, they were no match for Harrison's Kentuckians, and they surrendered. Proctor fled toward Moraviantown himself, leaving the Natives to continue the fight. This they did valiantly, until their leader Tecumseh was killed.

In case the British might decide to use Moraviantown as a base at another time, Harrison burned it down. Deciding not to advance any farther, he retreated with his troops down the Thames, leaving an American garrison at what was left of Fort Amherstburg. The Americans would begin almost immediately to rebuild the fort, renaming it Fort Malden.

The British had occupied Detroit from late August 1812 until September 1813, and now Harrison left American brigadier general Duncan McArthur in charge there. The American occupation of the Michigan Territory and western Upper Canada would continue until the end of the war.

De Rottenburg considered abandoning everything west of Kingston, the setback had been so severe. But Proctor had gathered 246 of his soldiers who had escaped after the battle and assembled them at Ancaster.

When he received the news of the British defeat at the Battle of Moraviantown, General Vincent, who was at Twenty Mile Creek, destroyed stocks and arms and hurried his men back to Burlington Heights. Like Proctor at Ancaster, he and the other officers at Burlington Heights were determined to hold their ground in the Niagara Peninsula.

With the loss of their fearless leader, Tecumseh, the Natives became disheartened. The representatives of six tribes signed a ceasefire with Harrison at Detroit, thereby ending Native resistance to the Americans around Lake Erie. The whereabouts of the body of Tecumseh remains a mystery to this day. It is thought that his devoted followers took him away to an unknown place to bury him.

The British still held the island of Michilimackinac, a key outpost that guarded the route to fur country. And instead of trying to take that strategic location, with winter coming on,

Harrison moved with his regulars to Fort George, where the rest of the American troops from the Niagara frontier were holed up.

11

The Frontier Burns

In the autumn of 1813 the snow came early, beginning in October, obliterating much of the evidence of the war's destruction, and staying on the ground for the rest of the winter. There was little left of any value after the Americans had pillaged the Niagara Peninsula, and no other part of the country had been so badly damaged by the war. Even what little firewood the settlers had cut in readiness for the cold weather had been stolen. All able-bodied young men were in the army or had been imprisoned in the United States. The only ones left to struggle through were women and children and old men.

The land itself had been ravaged by galloping hooves, wheels of heavy artillery wagons, and thousands of tramping feet. Bridges had been destroyed and roads torn to pieces. All through the area, the troops on both sides of the war had set up camp, dug latrines, and ripped up the rail fences to use as firewood.

To make matters worse, bands of armed marauders galloped through the countryside at night. There were frequent skirmishes between groups of renegades from either side, making it unsafe for law-abiding citizens like the Secords to venture out after dark.

Of all the marauders who roamed the country none was more notorious than the Irishman Joseph Willcocks. Once a member of Upper Canada's legislative assembly, Willcocks had become a traitor, spying for the Americans and passing on information about British troop movements.

In 1813 he had raised a troop of armed men to fight on the side of the Americans. They called themselves the Canadian Volunteers. Conducting nightly raids, they stole cattle and household goods, set fire to barns and homes, captured supplies, encouraged the militia to desert, and made prisoners of those who refused — all this in an effort to weaken the province's defences.

Before leaving Upper Canada to become a colonel in the American army, Joseph Willcocks had been a resident of Newark (Niagara-on-the-Lake). There he had established his newspaper, *The Upper Canadian Guardian or Freeman's Journal*, which he had used as a forum for voicing his criticism of British authorities.

Willcocks had been an admirer of Major General Isaac Brock, had fought for the British side at Queenston Heights, and Brock had mentored the young man. But Brock's successor, General Roger Hale Sheaffe, had had no time for the likes of Joe Willcocks, and when it appeared as if the Americans were going to win the war, Willcocks and some of his friends went over to the enemy.

Willcocks and his troop had briefly kidnapped Thomas Merritt, the former commander of the Niagara Light Dragoons. Merritt's son, William Hamilton Merritt, the commander of the Provincial Dragoons where Charles Ingersoll was lieutenant, wanted desperately to capture the renegade. Although Thomas Merritt had been released and returned to his home in Shipman's Corners, his son continued to try to track down Joseph Willcocks.

Late in 1813, the Americans made two attempts to invade Lower Canada, intent on taking Montreal.

On October 17, Major General James Wilkinson, who had taken over for General Dearborn, left Sackets Harbor, New York, with a flotilla of bateaux, the first part in a plan to follow the St. Lawrence route to Montreal. After a heavy gale and a freakish snowstorm the vessels were stranded at Grenadier Island in Lake Ontario, just eighteen miles from their starting point. Some of the boats had been badly damaged, the rations had been lost, and 196 of the men were so sick that Wilkinson sent them back to Sackets Harbor.

Map of the Niagara Frontier. From Benson J. Lossing, The Pictorial Field Book of the War of 1812.

Finally, on November 5, in brilliant sunshine, six thousand men in 350 boats, a procession five miles long, started down the St. Lawrence. British captain William Howe Mulcaster, Commander Yeo's second-in-command, with 650 men under Lieutenant Colonel Joseph Morrison, were in close pursuit. Morrison was leading his own 89th Regiment and a badly reduced 49th — the original Green Tigers who had fought from Queenston to Stoney Creek.

Although he was already four days behind schedule, Wilkinson suddenly stopped his flotilla. Ahead were the guns of the British at Fort Wellington in Prescott. He was expected to rendezvous at St. Regis, opposite Cornwall, with Major General Wade Hampton, who was following the Lake Champlain route to Montreal. But at Ogdensburg, Wilkinson ordered the boats unloaded, and in the night they slipped quietly downriver past Fort Wellington, unnoticed. When they were far enough away, the troops re-embarked.

Not surprisingly, since this was Loyalist country, the settlers all along the Canadian shore kept firing at the American boats from every bend in the river.

On November 8, the Americans reached the Long Sault rapids. They had been joined by Colonel Winfield Scott, who had left his own brigade back at Fort George and ridden thirty miles in heavy sleet through northern New York state to reach them.

The British forces under Morrison had disembarked from their own boats at Prescott, where they were joined by 240 men from the garrison. They marched along the banks of the St. Lawrence to arrive on November 10 at John Crysler's farm.

The farmhouse on the highway that ran along the riverbank provided Morrison with a good defensive position should the Americans tire of the chase down the St. Lawrence and turn to face him. His force of regulars, Canadian militia, and Mohawk allies was greatly outnumbered by the Americans, and so he was not looking for a pitched battle.

Colonel Winfield Scott had ordered Brigadier General Jacob Brown to clear the banks of the river of Canadian militia, so that the American boats could navigate the rapids without the threat of being fired upon. But when Wilkinson became aware of the British on Crysler's field he decided to destroy Morrison's small force there, before moving on.

At 8:00 a.m. on November 11 an alarm sounded. A Native had fired on an American patrol, but each side thought that the other had begun the attack. Morrison positioned the militia and Native warriors in the woods on either side of Crysler's field, and had the British regulars in two lines. A violent rainstorm had turned the deeply ploughed fields into ankle-deep mud. The American troops, who lost a number of senior officers early on, became disorganized. Their artillery, having been hauled back off the boats, was late in arriving, and try as they might, they weren't able to outmanoeuvre Morrison's troops. Their whole line began giving way, and eventually they left the battlefield.

When it was over, Morrison reported losses of twenty-two men killed, 148 wounded, and nine missing. The Americans reported 102 killed, 237 wounded, and over one hundred missing.

Along the north shore of the St. Lawrence the barns, stables, root cellars, and even the homes of many settlers, including that of John Crysler, had been plundered. Their rail fences had been torn up, their cattle taken, and their crop of winter wheat destroyed. The local population had no way of knowing that there never would be an American attack on Montreal, and so could take no comfort from that.

By the time Wilkinson's army stopped at Cornwall on November 12, he learned that Hampton had been defeated at the Battle of Châteauguay back on October 25. Hampton would not be joining him for the invasion of Montreal. Instead, he was returning to Lake Champlain to wait for spring.

Winter was on the doorstep, the morale of Wilkinson's men was dismal, and he himself was desperately ill. He was looking for an excuse to end the campaign, although he blamed Hampton for its failure.

When Hampton had made his foray along the Châteauguay River in late October, his large force had been stopped by three hundred Canadian Fencibles, Canadian Voltigeurs (militiamen from Lower Canada), and Natives, all commanded by Lieutenant Colonel Charles-Michel de Salaberry. Behind them were 1,200 militiamen and 150 Natives under Lieutenant Colonel "Red" Macdonnell. Hampton had retreated. The battle had been won entirely by Canadians, both English- and French-speaking.

Back in the States, Jacob Brown was promoted to major general. In February 1814 he would take two thousand men to Sackets Harbor and continue the fight for the Niagara frontier.

With the failed attempts by the Americans to take Lower Canada, the British government was again able to focus its attention on the Niagara Peninsula and send troops on the offensive, under a new commanding general, Gordon Drummond, Governor General Prevost's second-in-command.

The only foothold the Americans had on the Niagara Peninsula at that time was Fort George. The new American commander, Brigadier General George McClure, a New York Militia officer, was determined to break out of the fort, move up the peninsula, and oust General John Vincent's army from Burlington Heights. But he had a problem. The term of service for the American militia was coming to an end, and many of McClure's men had already left for home, without waiting for their discharge.

Nonetheless, McClure began his advance. He had reached Shipman's Corners when Joseph Willcocks, acting on false information, warned him that about two to three thousand British troops — the entire British Army, in fact — was on its way to meet him. In truth, the size of the force under Colonel John Murray, the British Army's inspecting field officer, was closer to 1,600.

Given those odds, McClure decided it would be foolhardy to continue the advance. He had only a hundred regulars, plus Willcocks's hundred Canadian Volunteers. Instead, he decided to abandon Fort George and return to the other side of the Niagara River. But before he left, he would burn down the town of Newark.

On December 10, an American patrol galloped through the town, shouting at the residents that they had fifteen minutes to vacate their homes. In shock, people stumbled into the streets, carrying what little they had time to gather and setting it in the snow.

The soldiers rode up and down every street in Newark setting the houses on fire, and among them was Joseph Willcocks — putting a torch to the homes of his former neighbours, people he had represented in the legislature. Powerless, the people stood in the snow and cold and watched the flames spread from one building to the next, until the whole town was burning.

One resident, Mrs. William Dickson, sister-in-law of Robert Dickson, the Scot who lived among the Sioux Nation and who had led 130 Native warriors in the bloodless surrender of Fort

Michilimackinac by the Americans, was sick in bed at the time. Her husband, William, was a prisoner at Fort Niagara. Like others in the town who were unable to walk out of their homes on their own, Mrs. Dickson was carried out of her house, bed and all, and plunked down in the snow. In helpless horror she watched her home — the first brick house to be built in Newark — set ablaze. The fire consumed everything she owned — all her linens and fine furniture, and a library of over a thousand books that had been bought in England at great expense.

Another story tells of a woman who had grabbed all her money before she ran from her home, leaving everything else behind. But once she got outside, one of the invaders had snatched the money from her hand, leaving her penniless.

Many inhabitants fled for their lives into the cold to find shelter in the country or with friends in one of the smaller villages. If the first farmhouse they came to was full, they trudged on through the snow to the next. Some four hundred women and children walked as much as ten miles that night trying to find a place to shelter, some crouching out of the wind against chimneys, the lucky ones huddling together in root cellars. All the public buildings in Newark and two of the churches were also torched.

By the time Colonel Murray and William Merritt arrived on the scene, it was all over. Merritt wrote about the devastation in his *Memoirs*, "Nothing but heaps of coals and the streets full of furniture that the inhabitants were fortunate enough to get out of their houses, met the eye in all directions."

Blowing up the main magazine at Fort George and spiking the guns, the Americans retreated across the river to Fort Niagara. They left intact a new barracks and 1,500 tents.

Furious at the enemy's senseless action against innocent women and children in Newark, Lieutenant General Gordon

Drummond came down from York to help Colonel Murray plan a secret revenge attack on Fort Niagara.

The American government quickly let it be known that it had not authorized McClure's action. In his own defence, McClure said he'd burned Newark because he knew the British were going to invade Fort Niagara across the river, and he didn't want to leave them with comfortable billets. Considering the barracks and tents that were left behind, this was unconvincing. By then the army had lost confidence in McClure anyway, and he turned his command over to Major General Amos Hall.

In preparation for the attack on Fort Niagara, William Merritt and his dragoons spent several days collecting boats to be used to ferry the British across the river at midnight. When the time came, much to his disappointment, Merritt was too ill to take part in the assault.

Sixty-five Americans lost their lives that night and sixteen were wounded, all at the end of a British bayonet. The British lost six men. Besides taking more than three hundred prisoners, the British gained military supplies, blankets, clothing, and thousands of pairs of badly needed shoes. With the successful capture of Fort Niagara, Major General Phineas Riall, Vincent's replacement, crossed the river and invaded Lewiston, New York.

Within a week, citizens on the American side of the Niagara frontier had been warned to leave the area, and from Fort Niagara to Tonawanda Creek, including the towns of Youngstown and Manchester (Niagara Falls, New York), the region was reduced to smouldering rubble.

As the inhabitants were fleeing Buffalo, Cyrenius Chapin, the Green Tigers' old nemesis, rode up to face the British, waving a white flag. But Chapin had no official standing in the community and was himself taken prisoner, this time under heavy guard.

Chapin had earlier sent his two young daughters, ages nine and eleven, out of town to try to reach his farm in Hamburg, ten miles away. Although it would be some time before their father knew the fate of the girls, neighbours found them safe, warming themselves in front of a log fire in a tavern where other refugees had gathered. They had walked nearly ten miles through the snow.

When one elderly widow in Buffalo complained to the British about their cruel burning of her town, she was told, "We have left you with one roof, and that is more than the Americans left for our widows [at Newark] when they came over."

The burning of Buffalo on December 29 and the onset of cold weather brought an end to the campaign of 1813. Keeping a garrison at Fort Niagara, the rest of the British returned to Upper Canada. Very little had changed hands that year; the British held Michilimackinac Island and the Americans occupied the ruined fort at Amherstburg. On Lake Ontario and Lake Erie the navies on both sides of the conflict would spend the winter in the endless competition to see which one could construct the world's largest lake vessel.

12

The Final Battles

If the inhabitants of the Niagara Peninsula thought conditions in 1813 had been bad, 1814 would be even worse.

In February 1814, Lieutenant General Drummond asked the legislature for the right to confiscate the property of convicted traitors, for the right to enforce martial law when necessary, and for a denial of the right of habeas corpus in certain cases. All Americans living in Canada who refused to fight for the Crown were required to leave the country.

The government of Upper Canada, tired of American sympathizers among the local population, sent out orders to round up any traitors. In the uneasy climate that created, neighbours became suspicious of neighbours, and people were often afraid to speak to one another, for fear of having their words misinterpreted.

Back in November 1813, a band of traitors had been caught in a surprise attack on a house near Port Dover, on Lake Erie.

Although several had managed to escape, a number were killed in the ensuing fight, and eighteen alleged traitors were taken prisoner. Four would be hanged for treason in 1814.

With each new battle there were more wounded men to be cared for, and with army doctors in short supply, militiamen like James Secord had to be cared for by their families at home, putting an added strain on dwindling resources.

Farmers and small shop owners often weren't paid for the food, hay, or wood they sold to the government. Debts that had been incurred as much as eighteen months earlier by Brock's army had not been looked after. When the settlers refused to sell their goods to the army, the government proclaimed partial martial law to force them to do so.

Sometimes even the soldiers and militiamen themselves weren't paid on time. The militiamen began to desert, returning home where they were needed for spring planting. Everywhere, people were demanding payment for damages to their property caused by the war.

By mid-March, Major General Phineas Riall reported more and more men deserting the British garrison at Fort Niagara, as the discontent among the troops spread. He was counting on the British 103rd Regiment to provide him with reinforcements as soon as the ice melted in the Niagara River.

Lieutenant General Drummond, waiting at York for the reinforcements Britain had promised, was worried. He had no idea where, in 1814, the Americans would strike first, nor when. All he knew for sure was that they *would* return. He asked Governor General Prevost to send him more men, but there were none to spare.

Drummond made the decision to keep the main force of eight hundred regular soldiers at Burlington Heights. The rest of the army's five thousand men were thinly spread from York to Fort Erie and were too few to contain an enemy attack.

To fortify the Niagara frontier, the British built Fort Drummond, an earthen fort on top of Queenston Heights, and another, Fort Mississauga, on Lake Ontario, a small fortification meant to replace the damaged Fort George. Its earthen walls were built in the shape of a star, and the stones and bricks used in the construction of its tower had been salvaged from the burnt-out town of Newark.

On the American side, Major General Jacob Brown had come up with a plan to seize Fort Erie, considered to be the weakest point on the frontier, and then to take the strategically important bridge over Chippawa Creek (the Welland River) that divided the peninsula in two. No invading force could march up the frontier without first taking and holding that bridge. The next step in Brown's plan would be a march to Fort George, where he fully expected Chauncey's fleet would be waiting, ready to give him heavy support.

At five in the morning on July 3, 1814, the badly outnumbered British garrison at Fort Erie surrendered to the Americans and the enemy advanced toward Chippawa.

The settlement of Chippawa was at the southern end of the Portage Road that began at Queenston and bypassed Niagara Falls. The homes and properties of the residents of Chippawa had been plundered by raiding parties numerous times, and now there was little left of any value.

When the British under Phineas Riall dug in on the north side of Chippawa Creek, the women and children who lived south of the creek picked up what they could, crossed the bridge, and set up camp in the open field beyond the British lines.

The two opposing armies were now within a mile of each other. The American troops numbered six thousand men, among them Winfield Scott's brigade, one of the best-trained outfits in the American army.

Riall had underestimated the size and skill of the American force, and he hadn't sent for the 103rd, who were by then at Burlington Heights. He had thought the Americans would mount a two-pronged attack — at Chippawa, as well as at the southwest end of Lake Ontario, with Chauncey's fleet bombarding Newark. As a precaution, he had sent one of his regiments back to Queenston.

He had also assumed most of the American force was made up of volunteers, men who would likely retreat in the face of the direct attack he was about to undertake.

Riall sent the militia and the Mohawk under John Norton into the woods, while he prepared his regulars to cross the bridge and advance on Brown's army.

On July 5, in a battle that lasted less than two hours, Riall lost one-third of his force, including some of his best officers. When the Battle of Chippawa was over, the British troops retreated across the bridge, tearing up its planking as they went, and withdrew to their camp. The Americans did not choose to follow them.

William Merritt reached Chippawa that evening and discovered that the two armies occupied exactly the same positions they had the night before. The only difference was that over eight hundred men were dead, wounded, or missing. Merritt was furious that Riall had not waited for reinforcements, nor called out the militia from the surrounding area.

Three days later the British encampment received the frantic warning that the Americans were coming, swimming the creek farther upstream, and would soon outflank their position. The British retreated in haste along the Queenston Road, heading for Fort George. Brown's troops took over their abandoned camp, and then without delay pressed onward to occupy Queenston Heights.

Riall's situation was critical. He couldn't hope to hold Fort George in the face of a bombardment by Chauncey's fleet; its walls were already crumbling. Changing course, he marched the British forces to Burlington Heights. Once again the Niagara Peninsula was under American control.

How disheartening it must have been for the Secords and other loyal citizens of Queenston to discover the enemy once more on the Heights above their homes. On either side of the village the open fields were dotted with hundreds of tents of the American army.

The American commander, Brown, had rushed his army from Chippawa, expecting Chauncey's imminent arrival. After first taking Fort George, the Americans intended to move on to Burlington Heights. From there they would press on to York and Kingston where they would cut the vital connection between Montreal and Upper Canada and finally end the war.

But Chauncey didn't come. The commander of the American fleet was ill and unwilling to turn his ships over to a second-in-command. He also believed that his only mandate was to do battle with the British fleet, not to transport troops.

During this time, while the Americans occupied Queenston, the British Army in Upper Canada was steadily growing stronger. The war in Europe had come to an end back on March 31, when the allies had captured Paris, and Napoleon had given up. By July 1814, the British government was able to send fourteen regiments to bolster the forces in Upper Canada. The volunteer army strengthened, too, as farmers flocked to Burlington Heights and Twenty Mile Creek.

The civilian population had been harassing the American forces, becoming so hostile toward the occupiers that American troops under Colonel Isaac Stone rode into Loyalist St. Davids on July 19 and burned it to the ground.

This time it was Laura's turn to provide shelter for her family, and she and James took as many of their Secord relatives into their home in Queenston as they could.

The house where Laura and James had lived in St. Davids when they were first married was lost in the burning of the little village, as was Stephen Secord's home and gristmill. Major David Secord, James's older brother and the one for whom the settlement had been named, lost nearly everything: numerous residences, both clapboard and stone, two new barns, some log buildings, grain, livestock, and household furnishings. A heroic leader, Major David Secord and the 2nd Lincoln Militia had distinguished themselves at the Battle of Chippawa.

With the increased strength in the number of British troops, the odds had changed in the Niagara Peninsula in favour of the British. Brown's American army had been reduced to 2,600. He knew that without Chauncey's assistance he couldn't take Fort George. On July 24, 1814, Brown moved the American troops back to Chippawa, where he would concentrate on reinforcing the army.

Lieutenant General Drummond came down from York to take command. His deputy, Phineas Riall, hot on Brown's heels, had begun to gather the British troops at Lundy's Lane where it crossed the Portage Road. From this position on the hill he was able to keep an eye on the American camp at Chippawa.

The entire British force on the Niagara frontier, including

Drummond's detachment and another 1,200 men from Twelve Mile Creek, was at Lundy's Lane when the two sides met there on July 25, 1814.

Although Winfield Scott, commander of the American force, realized he was outnumbered, he didn't wait for Brown's army to arrive before going into battle.

There was no moon that hot summer night at Lundy's Lane, and throughout the battle that went on all around the church on the knoll, the men on both sides were seldom more than twenty yards apart. In the dark it was impossible to tell who was a friend and who was the enemy. The troops fired their muskets at close range and stabbed and clubbed to death men who were fighting for the same side. Both sides were receiving reinforcements, and there was much coming and going, while the dead and wounded lay beneath their feet.

It was after 11:00 p.m. when the carnage ended. By then, Brown had used every man; he had no reserves. When the Americans retreated, the British were too exhausted to follow them.

It had been the bloodiest battle of the war thus far, with 880 British officers and men dead, wounded, or missing. Scott's American troops had almost as many casualties, including over five hundred men from his own brigade. William Hamilton Merritt of the Provincial Dragoons was among the prisoners taken by the American army. He would remain a prisoner in Cheshire, Massachusetts, until the end of the war.

The next day, July 26, the Americans returned to Lundy's Lane to reconnoiter. After taking a look at the British camp, the guns on the knoll, and Drummond's army on the heights above the battlefield, the Americans knew they were still outnumbered and out-positioned, and they retreated to the safety of Fort Erie. Under the command of Brigadier General Edmund P. Gaines, who had replaced Brown, they began to build a much larger and more fortified camp there.

The British were determined to oust them. On August 14, after a week of ineffective bombarding of Fort Erie, using the guns brought from Fort George, Drummond decided to attack. Even after terrible losses — more than 900 men, one-third of his army — he kept up the assault. Still, the British were unable to dislodge the Americans from the fort.

Autumn was approaching, and with it the cooler weather, but neither side was prepared to give up. The war had reached a stalemate, although neither the British nor the Americans would admit it.

Drummond's troops were ill, and the number of desertions continued to grow. Everyone was sick and tired of this war. Drummond began to run low on ammunition, and on September 21, when the Americans managed to take out two of the three British batteries in a surprise attack, he gave up the siege of Fort Erie. He moved back to the original British position at Chippawa Creek. The Americans didn't have the strength to pursue them.

Then, miraculously, a boost came for the American side: On September 28, Brigadier General George Izard arrived at Batavia, New York, with four thousand experienced troops from Lake Champlain. Izard's plan was to drive the British garrison out of Fort Niagara, but the American commander wanted him to do battle with the British who were dug in at Chippawa. On October 10, Izard's army crossed the river.

Drummond's force was not strong enough to go on the offensive, and he begged Governor General Prevost to send him more men and supplies. If he had two more regiments he could force the Americans back across the river and finish the war in

Upper Canada. Why couldn't Commander James Lucas Yeo help him to accomplish this?

Yeo reluctantly agreed to carry some troops and provisions across the lake, but he refused to overload his new ship, the *St. Lawrence*. He would transport only a small number of troops, and the rest would have to slog through the mud on foot to get there.

The American Izard had counted on Chauncey's fleet in order to accomplish his plan to take Chippawa and move on to Burlington Heights and York. But with Yeo's superiority on Lake Ontario, Chauncey had retreated to the safety of Sackets Harbor and would not come out.

The weather grew steadily worse. Men on both sides were weak from dysentery. Drummond himself was sick now, and he asked to go home. Izard saw no reason to stay on the Canadian side of the border, and as soon as there was a break in the weather, he withdrew from Fort Erie and returned to the United States. By November 1, all the Americans were back on their own soil.

On November 5, Lieutenant General Gordon Drummond dispatched James FitzGibbon, the former leader of the Green Tigers, and at that time a captain in the Light Infantry, to ride to Fort Erie to see what was going on there. When FitzGibbon galloped through the gates of the fort, he found the place deserted. The Americans had dismantled everything of value, blown up their impregnable fort, and gone home.

It had been five months since the Americans had come ashore at Fort Erie and successfully dislodged the small British garrison there. In that time, neither side had gained or lost any territory, although on the American side of the Niagara frontier the British hung on at Fort Niagara. Thousands of men were dead, even more wounded — some crippled for the rest of their lives — and hundreds were in prison.

—*//*—

On the east coast of the United States the Royal Navy had been conducting raids and carrying out blockades for months, harassing the settlements on Chesapeake Bay. In August 1814, a British Army seized Washington, setting fire to the president's mansion (it would later be dubbed the White House when the building was repaired and given a coat of whitewash). Other public buildings, too, were set ablaze, including the Library of Congress. The burning of Washington was supposedly in retaliation for the burning of the legislature at York.

The story goes that President James Madison's wife, Dolley, heard the rumble of cannon and saw the flash of the rockets fired by the invaders, but she didn't leave the mansion because she was waiting for word from the president. When the message that she must go arrived at three in the afternoon, she fled, taking with her the original Declaration of Independence and a life-sized portrait of George Washington.

The Treaty of Ghent ending the War of 1812 was drawn up in Belgium and signed on Christmas Eve 1814, but it was over a month before the news reached North America. Under the terms of the treaty each side was to return all territories it had seized. The area south of the Great Lakes would belong to the Americans, and north of the lakes would belong to Canada.

On January 8, 1815, two weeks after the peace treaty was signed, the bloodiest battle of all was fought. It was also the most senseless.

A British Army, eight thousand strong and led by Major General Edward Pakenham, went into battle near New Orleans, at the strategic mouth of the Mississippi River, against Andrew

Jackson's army. It took less than a half-hour for the Americans to win the assault, killing and wounding two thousand British soldiers, including Pakenham, the brother-in-law of Wellington who'd defeated Napoleon at the Battle of Waterloo.

Britain had encouraged the battle in order to speed up the peace negotiations, believing that if it won it might be able to dictate better terms from the Americans. Tragically, none of the combatants knew that the war was already over; it had been too late to call off the Battle of New Orleans.

Under the terms of the treaty the British gave back Michilimackinac Island and Fort Niagara, and the Americans returned Fort Amherstburg, now Fort Malden, to Canada. The British negotiators of the peace treaty had failed to understand the importance of Michilimackinac. When the British commander there finally heard the news, in May 1815, he was desolate with grief. The British had held the position in the northwest for three years. Now the peace treaty had brought to an end the British fur trade in the Upper Mississippi.

Because they'd won the last battle, the Americans considered they'd won the War of 1812. Their country *had* proved its strength and gained respect for its independence.

On the other hand, the Canadians thought they were the victors because they'd kept the Americans from conquering their country. And because the British had not had to give up any territory — at least none that they considered important — they decided that they'd won.

In truth, the war ended in a stalemate. No boundaries were changed. Neither side won. But the Native people, especially those living south and west of Lake Erie, lost the most. The bitter truth was that the British had deceived them. They had expected a separate Indian nation, with Britain as their ally. And although they had been valuable participants in the War of 1812, they had been prevented by the Americans from being part of the peace negotiations. There were no hunting grounds left to which they could return.

13

Family Fortunes

Laura sat in the rocking chair beside the kitchen fire holding her baby daughter, Laura Ann, against her shoulder, rhythmically patting her back. Fan was hacking away at one of last summer's turnips that was destined for the soup pot, and on the opposite side of the table Charlotte was teaching six-year-old Appy how to form her letters. From the next room came the rumble of men's voices.

Mary paced, picking up her needlework and promptly setting it down again. "I wish I knew what they were saying in there." From the window she looked out at Harriet playing in the yard with Charles. William's horse was tethered to the front post where it nibbled the first new shoots of spring grass.

This agony of waiting! Thirty minutes ago Mary had met William at the door, had dodged his attempt to steal a kiss, taken his hat, and ushered him into the parlour. "Papa, Dr. Trumbull has arrived." Pulling the door shut behind her, she'd scampered, red-faced, back to the kitchen.

Born in Kilmorgan, County Sligo, Ireland, in 1764, William Trumbull was no stranger to the Secord house. He was an assistant surgeon with the 37th Regiment of Foot and had been stationed at Queenston over the winter. Earlier, he'd come to take a look at James Secord's injured knee and had given his opinion about it. It would be unwise, he determined, to try now to remove the musket ball that remained lodged there. However slowly, James was able to get about with the help of his walking stick, and William could not promise he'd be able to do even that much if he went ahead with the surgery.

After that first consultation, William began to come to the house on a regular basis, and it soon became obvious to the rest of the family that there was another reason for his visits — a growing attraction between the doctor and the Secords' eldest daughter.

"The water has boiled," Mary said. "Should I get the tea ready? It would help keep my mind off what Papa might be saying to William."

No one had been surprised when William had asked to come to talk to James, and Laura had a pretty good idea how the conversation in the next room was proceeding.

"She's very young," James would say.

"She is indeed, sir," William would undoubtedly reply. "And I will always do my best to take good care of her."

It would go much the same way as she knew the conversation between James and her own father, Thomas Ingersoll, had gone. Although in her case, Laura had been twenty-two and James just two years older.

Mary *was* young, only seventeen, and Trumbull thirty-five years her senior, older even than Laura and James themselves.

Had he not been posted, effective the next May, to Jamaica, where surgeons were needed, the couple might have waited for a few months, at least until Mary's eighteenth birthday.

When Laura and James had talked privately about the possibility of a spring wedding, Laura was already picturing the wedding gown she'd make for Mary. A skillful seamstress, Laura was adept at making dresses, slippers, and even gloves. Fifteen-year-old Charlotte, and Harriet, who had just turned thirteen, would need new gowns, and satin slippers to match, of course. (Although Harriet was likely to object to all the fussing.)

It would be wonderful to celebrate a happy occasion after two and a half long years of war. Not that the birth of Laura Ann at home in Queenston in October 1815 had not been a happy event.

On April 18, 1816, in a ceremony at Niagara Falls, Mary Secord married Dr. William Trumbull. For the wedding trip the couple sailed to Ireland to introduce Mary to the groom's parents, Harloe and Elizabeth Trumbull (in Ireland, also spelled Trumble).

In July 1815, the Secords had received the sad news that James's brother-in-law and former mentor, Richard Cartwright, who'd been married to James's sister Magdalene, had died in Montreal. He'd been a wealthy man, a well-respected political and religious leader in Upper Canada.

James Secord's store was among many in Queenston that had been left in ruins when the war ended, and his career as a merchant was officially over. He now counted on the rent from two hundred acres of land that he owned in Grantham Township to support his growing family. He hoped that his tenants would not be long in making their payments.

James and Laura had been heartened to learn that some of their old friends in Newark whose homes had been destroyed in the fires set by the Americans in 1813 would receive compensation from the Loyal and Patriotic Society. In better times, the Secords themselves had made small donations to this charity that depended on the generosity of Upper Canadians to carry on its work.

Reverend John Strachan, the rector of the Anglican parish at York, had founded the Loyal and Patriotic Society in 1812 to raise and distribute money to militiamen and their families who were suffering hardships due to the war.

During the winter of 1812–13, the society had provided warm clothing to the men serving along the Niagara River, and after the capture of York in April 1813 they had contributed funds for the medical care of the wounded British and Canadian forces, at a time when there was no British medical personnel available at York.

Women and children sometimes marched with their husbands and fathers during the War of 1812, and the Loyal and Patriotic Society had also provided travel expenses so that a couple of these women whose husbands had been killed in action could return to their homes.

There was another wedding in Laura's family in 1816. Her half-brother Charles Ingersoll married Anna Maria Merritt, the sister of his friend William Hamilton Merritt. Elizabeth Secord, Laura's niece who had accompanied her part of the way on her walk to Beaver Dams and who had been engaged to Charles, had died in 1814.

A year after his marriage, Charles bought the original tract of land in Oxford-on-the-Thames where his father had first settled, and in 1821, after building a fine house, he moved there with his family.

At the end of the war, Charles Ingersoll and William Merritt had formed a partnership in a mercantile business. It would fail, however, in 1819 because of some bad debts. Later, the two would manage to pay off their Montreal wholesalers.

Today, William Hamilton Merritt is best known as the idea man behind the Welland Canal that connected Lake Ontario to Lake Erie. Merritt enlisted the support of the government for the project, worked tirelessly to raise funds, and supervised the canal project. It officially opened for shipping on November 30, 1829. Even before the Welland Canal opened, Merritt had in his mind another canal, one that would bypass the rapids between Prescott and Lachine in the St. Lawrence River.

James and Laura's first grandchild, Elizabeth Trumbull, was born in Ireland on March 27, 1817, the same year as Laura herself gave birth to her seventh and last child. She and James named their baby girl Hannah Cartwright, in honour of Richard. Laura was forty-two.

Mary and William Trumbull had a second daughter, also called Mary, born in Jamaica around 1820. Sadly, William died a year later, and Mary and her two small daughters came home to Queenston, back into the arms of her family.

For three years following the war, the harvests from the ravaged countryside were meagre. Everyone had homes or shops that needed rebuilding, and Queenston itself was a wreck, with wharves and warehouses destroyed. The Secords had been fairly well-off before the war, but afterward their situation changed dramatically.

In 1817, in order to support his family, James had to sell six lots he owned in Queenston. As did the heads of many households, James Secord submitted a claim to the government for possessions he'd lost to the British and American forces. He asked for an amount to cover the furnishings of a twenty-by-sixteen-foot room, as well as a porch, a stable, his storehouse and shelving, chimneys, wagons, and other materials. He had not expected compensation for the total amount, and the £485 he did receive gave a boost to the coffers of his expanding family.

Gradually the yield from the local fruit and vegetable crops began to increase, and milk returned to the kitchens in the Niagara Peninsula. Still, the new flock of chickens in Laura's yard was slow to lay eggs, meat remained scarce, and even necessities like flour and salt were exorbitantly priced.

The time came when Laura's daughter Mary decided that it would be best if she and the children went back to Ireland, where there would be a good pension from William's service to the British Army for her and the girls. William's parents and large extended family were all urging her to return. The Secords' second daughter, Charlotte, went to Ireland with her sister in order to help her with the little ones during the long voyage.

One source suggests that Charlotte Secord may have been in love with a lieutenant who, like William Trumbull, had also died in Jamaica. If that was the case, the sisters' mutual grief would have created an even stronger bond between them. Charlotte, who would never marry, remained in Ireland with Mary for some time, made most welcome by her sister's in-laws. She would help Mary raise the oldest girl, Elizabeth, before returning to her own family in Upper Canada.

After the War of 1812, many people in Upper Canada needed the help of the British Crown in order to rebuild their lives, and the usual way to get it was to petition the lieutenant-governor of the province. As previously mentioned, James Secord petitioned for a licence to operate a stone quarry on military land near Queenston in 1820. As well as mentioning in the petition that he was the brother-in-law of the late Honourable Richard Cartwright, and recounting his own service in the Battle of Queenston Heights and the injuries he'd received there, he also mentioned Laura's heroic contribution to the war. Laura had asked Lieutenant James FitzGibbon to provide a certificate in support of James's petition, which he had done (previously cited). The contents of the petition were confidential, of course, and the public was still unaware of Laura's heroism.

As it turned out, James was successful in getting the rights to operate the stone quarry, but following the war the market for stone was limited, and the enterprise did not provide as much money for his family as James had hoped.

After another petition to Lieutenant-Governor Sir Peregrine Maitland, the government's medical board granted James a pension, declaring him "incapable of earning his livelihood in consequence of wounds received in action with the Enemy" at the Battle of Queenston Heights. The pension was small, only £18 per year (about $50), but it was something.

On November 23, 1824, the Secords' third daughter, Harriet, married St. Catharines lawyer David William Smith, the son of wealthy farming parents who lived in Fort Erie. The couple would subsequently have three children: Laura Louisa, Mary Augusta, and William James.

Early in 1827, James Secord petitioned the government for some sort of employment for himself. Instead of giving James a job, Maitland suggested a position for Laura. How would she feel about being put in charge of Brock's monument at Queenston Heights when it was finished? At first Laura turned it down, but later she changed her mind.

Maitland may have been a personal friend of the Secords. He was said to have had "a favourable opinion of the character and claims of Mr. Secord and his wife."

Back in 1815 the government had allowed for a monument to be built to commemorate Major General Sir Isaac Brock's service to the country. The members of the monument committee were Colonel Thomas Clark, Thomas Dickson, and Lieutenant Colonel Robert Nichol, all veterans of the war. In 1820, a 135-foot column was erected near the spot at Queenston Heights where Brock had died. Inside the column was a spiral staircase leading to an observation deck, and there was a square room at the base of the monument to be used as a visitors' lobby.

Although not yet completed, the monument was dedicated in 1824 on the twelfth anniversary of Brock's death, and the bodies of Sir Isaac Brock and Lieutenant Colonel John Macdonell were removed from Fort George in a solemn ceremony. Thousands gathered to watch the procession as the black-draped hearse drawn by four black horses, the dignitaries, and the chiefs of the Six Nations made their way slowly from the fort to the monument at Queenston Heights where the bodies of the two war heroes were placed in a vault. Lining the route of the procession were members of the Lincoln Militia. If James Secord was not there with his fellow militiamen in person, he was surely there in spirit.

On June 1 there was another ceremony, this one to lay the cornerstone of Brock's monument. William Lyon Mackenzie, who had recently opened his newspaper office in Queenston, was asked to provide some items that might be suitable to put in a time capsule, a sealed bottle beneath the cornerstone. Among the mementos he chose was an issue of his newspaper that carried an article he had written, critical of the lieutenant-governor. When Sir Peregrine Maitland heard of this affront, he had the cornerstone dug out and the offending *Colonial Advocate* removed.

James Secord had twice written letters to Lieutenant-Governor Maitland stressing the dire financial straits in which he found himself. Before Maitland was transferred to Nova Scotia in 1828, he responded to James's requests for a position by appointing him Registrar of the Niagara District Surrogate Court. For her part, Laura was hoping the new lieutenant-governor of the province, Sir John Colborne, would honour Maitland's promise to her, and put her in charge of Brock's monument when it was finally completed.

Her duties there would include collecting admission, showing visitors around the site, and providing refreshments from the bar. She began eagerly anticipating her new employment, hoping that along with James's position it would bring an end to their financial troubles.

In 1828 one of the Secords' trusted servants, reportedly Fan, died of cholera. They could not afford to replace her. At the end of the same year the family suffered a devastating blow. On December 20, James and Laura lost their eighteen-year-old daughter Appy (Appolonia) to typhus.

One day in 1829 Laura took some visiting relatives to view Brock's monument. One can imagine her telling her guests as she showed them around that soon she would be in charge of the attraction that was drawing more tourists all the time.

She and her relatives signed the guest book that day in September. Laura's signature was there, as well as that of her step-mother, Sally Ingersoll, and a niece, Mary Ann Ingersoll, of Oxford County, Laura's daughter, Mary Trumbull, and Laura's three-year-old granddaughter, Laura Louisa Smith.

While Laura was still waiting for word about her position, one of the members of the monument committee was killed in a tragic accident. During a freak snowstorm in May, Robert Nichol became lost on his way home to Stamford, and he and his horse and cart went over the precipice at Queenston. Nichol was survived by his widow and four small children. The family was left destitute. Given this unfortunate turn of events, Thomas Clark, the only member of the original monument committee still living, advised the new lieutenant-governor to give the position of caretaker of Brock's monument to someone who really needed it — Nichol's widow.

Getting wind of this, Laura sent an urgent letter to Lieutenant-Governor Colborne reminding him of Maitland's promise to her, but Colborne refused to step in on her behalf, and in 1831 the key to the monument was turned over to Mrs. Nichol. Laura was bitterly disappointed.

"It's out of your hands now," James told her gently.

If only she hadn't counted on it so much!

"What is it you always say, my dear?" James reminded her. "That God will take care of us?"

Never one to give up easily, on July 17, 1831, Laura wrote an angry letter to the new lieutenant-governor's secretary. She told him, in no uncertain terms, that Maitland had said to Colonel Clark that "it was too late to think of Mrs. Nichol as I have pledged my word to Mrs. Secord that as soon as possible she should have the key."

As further proof of her worthiness for the position, Laura attached to her letter a copy of a certificate written by Lieutenant James FitzGibbon on March 11, 1827, in which he confirmed the significance of her heroic walk — her communication with him the evening of June 22, 1813, which was the day before the

American troops left Fort George. It had been because of her information that FitzGibbon had been able to place his forces in the best position before the Americans arrived. And after the Natives had confirmed Laura's information that the enemy was indeed advancing on Beaver Dams, they, too, had been fully prepared for the battle on June 24, 1813.

But it was all of no use. Someone else had been given the coveted position as caretaker of Brock's monument.

There was more to come in the saga of the monument. As one of the closing acts of the Rebellion of 1837, an explosive charge was set off in the base of Brock's monument on April 17, 1840, causing serious damage to the structure. It was believed that one of William Lyon Mackenzie's supporters, Benjamin Lett, was responsible for the destruction. The remains of the two fallen heroes, Brock and Macdonell, had to be removed, and they were temporarily buried in the Hamilton family cemetery in Queenston.

In 1856, a second monument, the one you see today at Queenston Heights, was finished. Built entirely of cut stone, the monument is 185 feet (fifty-six metres) high. Among the names of the committee authorized to erect this second monument were the Honourable William Hamilton Merritt and Colonel Robert Hamilton, the man who had founded Queenston.

The bodies of Brock and Macdonell were returned to their final resting place in a vault beneath the monument. Inside the monument are tributes to the men of the British, Canadian, and First Nations forces who died at Queenston Heights.

A plate attached to Brock's coffin reads:

Here lie the earthly remains of a brave and virtuous hero, Major General Sir Isaac Brock, commander of the British forces, and president administering the government of Upper Canada, who fell when gloriously engaging the enemies of his country, at the head of the flank companies of the 49th regiment in the town of Queenston, on the morning of the 13th October, 1812, aged 42 years.

14

The Move to Chippawa

"Your sister Laura never had better health," James Secord wrote in a letter to his sister-in-law Mira Ingersoll Hitchcock in December 1829. "She bears her age [Laura was 54] most remarkably considering her former delicate state of body.... We are however, Mira, getting old and grey heads, and now and then a tremor of the body.... With respect to our worldly affairs I am sorry to say we are not very prosperous. We make out to live and have clothing and food, but riches, my dear woman, it seems to me, is not for James Secord ..."

Although she had married Julius Hitchcock in Upper Canada sometime before 1807, Mira and her husband were living back in Massachusetts when this letter was written.

It may have been a Christmas letter, bringing Laura's sister up-to-date on the latest news of the Secord family. Mira was the only one of Laura's three sisters, daughters of Thomas Ingersoll and his first wife, Elizabeth (Betsy) Dewey, still living at this time. The second daughter, Elizabeth, had died in 1811 at the age of thirty-two, and the youngest, Abigail, who'd been raised in the United States by the Nash family, had died when she was thirty-eight, in 1821.

In 1833, James received a promotion from registrar to judge of the Niagara District Surrogate Court that had jurisdiction over the wills and estates of deceased persons. It was the same position that had been held by the ill-fated Robert Nichol.

With James's promotion, the Secords' twenty-four-year-old son, Charles Badeau, stepped in to replace his father in the position of registrar. Earlier, because James's ability to get around was very limited, Charles had assumed the job of collecting the rent from his father's land tenants upon which James and Laura depended. The young man was also studying to become an attorney-at-law. On November 26, 1830, at the age of twenty-one, Charles had married Margaret Ann Robins of Kingston.

Laura's beloved half-brother Charles Ingersoll had died in a widespread cholera epidemic in 1832, leaving his widow, Anna Merritt Ingersoll, and eight children. A year later, Laura's step-mother, Sally Whiting Ingersoll, died after a long illness, at the age of seventy-one.

Always looking to better himself and to provide for his family, James resigned his judge's position in the Surrogate Court in 1835 to become Collector of His Majesty's Customs at the Port of Chippawa. Although he would receive no salary from this job, he would be entitled to a percentage of the fees on goods going through the port and to a share in the seizures he made of any smuggled items.

At the age of sixty-two, James Secord had won the position over a field of more than a dozen applicants. For a while it turned out to be the best-paying job he'd ever had, and the couple began to live a little more comfortably.

The job came with a good house, and in 1835 James and Laura left Queenston and moved into the Customs House at Chippawa. Their son Charles took over the family home in Queenston, where he would continue to be responsible for collecting the rent from James's land tenants.

Chippawa, situated three miles above Niagara Falls, had long been an important trading centre, located as it was at the end of the Portage Road that bypassed the rapids and falls. However, with the completion of the first Welland Canal in 1829, ships with cargo destined for points farther west no longer had to unload at Queenston and be transported overland to Chippawa.

Now, teams of horses and oxen moved along tow roads on either side of the canal, pulling the schooners from one lock to the next and finally into safe water.

The idea for the canal likely grew out of William Hamilton Merritt's need to provide water from Chippawa Creek (the Welland River) to run his mills at Twelve Mile Creek. From there it developed into a plan to connect Lake Ontario to Lake Erie.

The canal began at Port Dalhousie on Lake Ontario and ran along Twelve Mile Creek to Port Robinson where it connected with Chippawa Creek, went past the village, and on to the Niagara River, exiting into Lake Erie.

By 1833, several modifications had been made, and the canal was at that time twenty-seven miles long (forty-three kilometres) and had forty wooden locks. In 1839 the Welland Canal would begin to route traffic through Port Colborne, and eventually Niagara Falls would become the region's port of customs. Although later canal routes would bypass Chippawa, while James and Laura Secord lived there in the 1830s, the village enjoyed prosperous times.

On May 9, 1833, Laura and James's first grandson was born to Charles and Margaret. They named him Charles Forsyth Secord. A second son, James Badeau, would be born to the couple in 1836, and in 1838 a daughter, Alicia, arrived.

Charles Forsyth Secord would one day become a professor, teaching in what is today Niagara Falls, Ontario. In 1865 he and his family would move to Nebraska and later to Iowa. Although both James and Alicia would marry, neither would have any children.

According to genealogist and Niagara-area historian David F. Hemmings, in his book *Laura Ingersoll Secord, A Heroine and Her Family* (Bygones Publishing, Niagara-on-the-Lake, 2010), Charles Forsyth Secord's is the only surviving line of (James) Secords alive today.

Before Laura and James moved to Chippawa there had been two more weddings in their family: the youngest daughter, Hannah Cartwright Secord, married Hawley Williams, a settler from Guelph, on April 22, 1833, in Queenston. And later that same year, on October 17, also in Queenston, Laura Ann married Captain John Poore.

It often seemed to the average person in Upper Canada that the people who ran the government were like members of a powerful family, a "compact" that made sure that the best land for developing and all the government jobs went only to their friends and relatives. One of the ties uniting this group was the loyalty they'd shown to Britain during the War of 1812.

William Lyon Mackenzie was a Scot who had come to Canada in 1821, and for a while he had run a general store in Dundas.

This Family Compact rankled Mackenzie and he decided the most effective way for him to show his opposition to it was through his writing. To this end he had opened his newspaper office in Queenston in 1824, publishing the *Colonial Advocate.*

Six months later, he moved his printing presses to York, where he would be nearer the seat of government. The move came as a relief to many Loyalists in Queenston, including James Secord, who, based on Mackenzie's writings, considered the man a traitor.

At York, Mackenzie set about exposing the dishonest way in which government money was being spent. He published lists of who was on the government's payroll, who they were related to, and exactly how much each one of them was being paid.

In retaliation, a gang of wealthy young hoodlums broke into Mackenzie's home where his newspaper office was, wrecked his printing press, and threw all the type into Lake Ontario. Because the vandals were sons of powerful families, no official tried to stop the attack. Mackenzie managed to sue, and he was awarded enough damages that he could buy new equipment and start up his paper again.

He decided to try to get elected to the assembly and ran as a Reformer in the 1827 election, easily winning the county of York. In 1830 he was re-elected, although many other Reformers lost their seats. It appeared as if people found less to complain about under Lieutenant-Governor Sir John Colborne.

The fiery Mackenzie, however, got worked up about every little thing. In December 1831 the Tory majority expelled him from the legislature. He won a by-election a few weeks later, and his supporters gave him a gold medal and a victory parade. In less than a week, he was again expelled.

After being mugged and having garbage thrown at him, Mackenzie and his wife fled to England, where he took the

Reformers' grievances to officials of the government there. Colborne was ordered to allow him back into the assembly.

In March 1834, York, now called Toronto, became a city and William Lyon Mackenzie won the first race for the mayor's chair. He was elected to parliament again at the end of 1834, but lost his seat in the assembly in 1836. Embittered, he started another newspaper, the *Constitution*, in which he vented his frustrations. He even began hinting that people might have to take up arms against the government.

In December 1837, hundreds of men led by Reformer Samuel Lount began gathering at Montgomery's Tavern north of Toronto. Mackenzie had planned for a show of force for December 7, but on December 5 the rebels took matters into their own hands and began to march down Yonge Street. They were met by a group of about twenty well-armed Loyalist guards, who shot at them. When it was over, two rebels and one guard lay dead. The following day a force of about a thousand Loyalists marched on Montgomery's Tavern and the rebels fled.

Mackenzie and a few of his followers escaped to Niagara where, disguised as a woman, he crossed to the American side of the river. With American support he took over Navy Island, planning to use it as a base for launching attacks on Upper Canada in order to free it from British rule.

Navy Island in the Niagara River was just opposite the village of Chippawa. Here he set up his provisional government, and hoisted his Republic of Canada flag, bearing the two stars that represented Upper and Lower Canada.

The citizens of Chippawa watched with growing alarm as the ship, the *Caroline*, based at Fort Schlosser on the American side of the river, moved day after day between the island and the American mainland, carrying men and supplies to the rebels.

Government of Ontario Art Collection, 621229.

The March of the Rebels upon Toronto in December, 1837.
Artist C.W. Jefferys.

During the night of December 29, a group of Loyalists led by Royal Navy Commander Andrew Drew, rowed across the river, cut the *Caroline* loose, and set her on fire. The burning vessel drifted into the current in the river, where it was swept over the falls in a mass of flames.

James Secord had been eager to be part of the adventure, fearing as he did that within a month the growing rebel force on the nearby island could mean trouble for the citizens of Chippawa and beyond.

Asked for his assistance, James had kept a fire burning that night at the mouth of Chippawa Creek, providing a light to guide the Loyalists' boats to and from the opposite shore of the Niagara River.

After the loss of the *Caroline*, Mackenzie finally abandoned the island on January 14, 1838; the weather was cold and his supplies were dwindling. He sought refuge in the United States, although his followers continued sporadic raids on Chippawa, even setting the frame Anglican Church of the Holy Trinity that the Secords attended on fire the night of September 12, 1839.

Only after the murder of a resident of Chippawa, said to have helped pilot the boats that had been involved in the burning of the *Caroline*, did the raids by the rebels end. A new Anglican church, built of red brick, replaced the first, and the cornerstone was laid by Bishop John Strachan in 1841.

Mackenzie spent the next twelve years in exile in the United States, where he became a correspondent for the *New York Daily Tribune* and wrote a number of books. He was pardoned by the Canadian government and allowed to return to Toronto in 1849, starting a new newspaper and running in the next election for a seat in the parliament of the new province of Canada — a union of Upper and Lower Canada that had been proclaimed by the Crown on February 10, 1841.

He resigned from politics in 1858, in debt and frustration. Thanks to the kindness of his friends, he spent the last three years of his life with his family in a furnished house provided by his supporters. William Lyon Mackenzie died in 1861.

There was always an element of danger for James Secord as the Collector of Customs at the Port of Chippawa. Smugglers often tried to get goods past customs without paying the duty on them.

One day James got word that a pair of smugglers was expected to make an attempt to land on the Canadian side of the river at a certain time. He and his deputy collector, a man named John, made plans to be there when the boat came in and to try to persuade the smugglers to surrender their goods.

When Laura got wind of the plan she insisted that James get more help. "There are only two of you," she pointed out, "and there is great danger."

She persuaded James to let her go along, disguised as a third man. Donning one of James's coats, and a hat, and pulling on a pair of his long boots, she went with them to intercept the smugglers. Having a third "man" lurking in the background gave the two customs officers the advantage they needed and the plan went off without a hitch.

Unfortunately, the potential for James to earn a lot of money as a customs collector at Chippawa was never fully realized. With the uprising of Mackenzie's Rebellion of 1837 and the frequent rebel attacks on Chippawa his income instead declined.

The couple must also have been contributing toward the support of their daughters and grandchildren from time to time. Ever since Laura Ann's husband, Captain John Poore, died in 1837, she and her two-year-old son, John Jr., had been living with James and Laura in the Customs House. Captain Poore had died shortly after raising a militia battalion in Hamilton for service during the 1837 Rebellion.

Daughter Harriet's husband, David William Smith, was an alcoholic, and the Secords' youngest daughter, Hannah, and her farmer husband, Hawley Williams, were having a constant struggle to make ends meet.

Late in 1839, Laura sent a petition to the lieutenant-governor asking for the concession that had recently become vacant to run the ferry between Queenston and Lewiston. She and James may have considered the ferry concession as less stressful employment for James, whose health was beginning to deteriorate. They were prepared to take Laura Ann and her son and move back to Queenston in order to get the better position.

It was customary with these documents for the petitioner to stress the loyalty of himself and his family, and Laura began her petition by telling the story of her service to her country at Beaver Dams in 1813. She attached a certificate written for her by Colonel FitzGibbon in 1837, attesting to her walk of "about 20 miles partly though the woods."

She wrote that she

> did at great Risk, peril and danger travelling on foot & partly at Night by a circuitous rout[e], through woods, mountains, enemy's lines and Indian Encampments to give important intelligence of a meditated attack by the Americans upon our troops & by which means 550 of the enemy were captured with two field Pieces and which circumstance has been the foundation of a desease [*sic*] from which the foes never recovered and for which performance [she] has never Received the smallest compensation being now informed that the Ferry at Queenston is unoccupied she your Memorialist will take your Excellency's Memorialist Case into Kind consideration & grant her the Ferry at Queenston for a term of years, say from 7, 14 or 21 years.
>
> Your Excellency's Memorialist would not now presume to ask any remuneration but from the circumstance of having a large family of Daughters and Grand-Daughters to provide for & for which the small means of Husband Captain James Secord Sen'r ...

Laura Secord did not get the Queenston ferry concession. She tried again in 1840 when Governor General Lord Sydenham took over and she heard the position was still vacant. This petition, too, was denied.

After that, Laura's life changed forever. Her beloved James suffered a stroke and died at home in Chippawa on February 22, 1841, at the age of sixty-seven.

15

The Widow Carries On

Laura honoured James's wishes that he be buried in the Drummond Hill (Niagara Falls) cemetery where the bloody Battle of Lundy's Lane had been fought in 1814, and where so many of his fellow Lincoln County militiamen lay buried.

The Reverend William Leeming, who conducted the funeral service at the Anglican Church of the Holy Trinity in Chippawa, said of James Secord, "[He] was a conscientious and upright man, amiable in all the relations of his life, a kind husband, an indulgent parent, a sincere friend and an obliging neighbour."

How many of the Secords' six surviving children attended the funeral is unknown. The oldest daughter Mary lived in Ireland, but the others would surely have been there.

Laura was sixty-five when James died, and with his death his small war pension came to an end. Later that year she wrote to her sister Mira, "You cannot think what grief we are in." Not only had she lost her life's companion, she now had to find a way to support herself. Widows' pensions were unheard of in those days.

The neighbours in Chippawa came to call on Laura, with offers of friendship along with their condolences. She had always been a little reserved, and much as she appreciated their kindnesses in her time of grief, she still preferred to keep to herself.

The first thing Laura did was to write a petition to Governor General Lord Sydenham to request that her son Charles be appointed collector of customs to succeed his father.

She wrote:

> [Her] late husband held in his lifetime the office of Collector of Customs for Port Chippawa which becoming vacant by his death has left your Memorialist without any means of support with two daughters and several grandchildren depending entirely on her. Your Memorialist has moved into this Province from the United States of America during the Revolutionary War and was all her life a firm supporter of the British Sovereign which the whole County will attest.
>
> That your Memorialist has ... ventured to apply to your Excellency for the appointment of Collector for her only son Charles that he will render her much assistance.
>
> Laura Secord
> Chippawa
> 27th Feb'y 1841

Charles had already succeeded James in the position of registrar of the Niagara Surrogate Court in 1835 and was now a practising attorney-at-law. However, Laura's petition was denied. Unlike the former lieutenant-governor, Sir Peregrine Maitland, Governor General Sydenham did not have the same appreciation for how much James and Laura Secord had contributed in service to their country.

In May 1841, Laura sent another petition asking, for the first time, for a pension for herself. Previously she'd petitioned for an appointment or a concession, but never for money.

Once again Sydenham denied Laura's request, stating, "The Petitioner's late Husband enjoyed up to his death a pension of twenty pounds [it was actually eighteen] for his wound, besides holding the Situation of Collector of Customs at Chippawa."

Two months later, Sydenham himself was dead.

In November 1841, possibly with financial help from her daughters Charlotte and Harriet and other more well-off members of her extended family, Laura bought a small house on Water Street (later named Bridgewater St.) on the banks of Chippawa Creek. It was an 1837-style cottage, originally owned by James Cummings, the son of Thomas Cummings, who in 1783 had been the first settler in Chippawa. Built of red brick, the cottage had a latticed porch where Laura would later grow climbing roses. From the window of her new home she had a view of the bridge that connected the two sides of the village.

When Harriet's husband, lawyer David William Smith, died of alcohol poisoning in May 1842, a little over a year after James's death, Harriet's three children were left without a father. Before moving from Queenston to Chippawa, Laura and James had seen a lot of these three grandchildren, who lived in nearby St. Catharines.

Harriet and her two daughters, Laura Louisa, aged sixteen, and Mary Augusta, about ten, came to live with Laura in her Water Street house in Chippawa. They would remain there with her for the rest of Laura's life, her constant companions.

Harriet's only son, William James, who would have been about twelve at the time of his father's death, went to live with his father's parents, the Smiths, on their farm in Fort Erie. Grandfather Smith died a year and a half later, and young William remained on the farm where he was raised by his grandmother.

By 1856, William James Smith had immigrated to the United States, where he married Elizabeth Bresnahan and had five sons. One source states that William was running a grocery store in Chicago in 1857 and later worked as an accountant in Prescott, Wisconsin.

For a time Laura ran a day school in her Chippawa home, teaching a few local children the three Rs. Although not trained as teachers, many colonial women made a meagre living for themselves in this way, charging a small fee from the parents of their students.

Laura Secord's school-teaching days were short-lived, however. The union of Upper and Lower Canada eventually saw the establishment of the publicly-supported common school system that guaranteed elementary education for all children in Canada.

The Chippawa cottage would have been bursting at the seams by the time Laura Ann, who had lived with her parents and her small son since the 1837 death of her husband, Captain John Poore, remarried on July 11, 1843. Her second husband, whom she married in Guelph, was Dr. William Clarke, an Irish physician. Their first child, William, born in 1844, lived only a year, as did their last child, Millicent, who was born in 1849. The couple's middle child, Laura Secord Clarke, born October 23,

1846, in Guelph lived until May 1936, in her ninetieth year. Laura Ann's son John Poore from her first marriage also lived on into the twentieth century.

Dr. William Clarke held several public service positions during his lifetime, was a member of parliament, and in 1864–65 served as the mayor of Guelph. Laura Ann herself had died in 1852, at the age of only thirty-seven.

Harriet's two daughters, who lived with their mother and grandmother, never married. They were both artists, and over the years they taught drawing, watercolours, and leather work in select schools for girls.

Even though her home was often filled with the younger generations of her family, Laura suffered bouts of loneliness. She longed to see her sister Mira, writing to her, "My dear Sister, how often I wish I could be near you and tell you all my griefs. I feel so lonely …"

Massachusetts felt like such a long way from Chippawa. Laura would outlive her younger sister Mira by more than twenty years. Her religious faith that grew stronger as she grew older helped Laura get through the early years of her widowhood.

Laura's granddaughter, whose married name was Alicia Secord Cockburn, the daughter born in 1838 to Charles and Margaret Ann Secord, described her grandmother as she knew her in later life as "a woman of strong personality and character and her word carried weight with it…. She was a great favourite with young people who, on returning home from school for their holidays would say, after only a short time at home, 'now we must go and see Mrs. Secord.'"

Harriet's daughter Laura Louisa Smith also referred to the way the neighbours, especially the young children, adored her grandmother. Ever since her earliest days, when she was little more than a child herself and had been charged with the care of her younger siblings, Laura had had a special connection with children. Some sources mention how this new generation of children loved to hear Laura tell stories of her early life.

It is possible, since she was skilled at dressmaking and needlework, that Laura made a little money sewing for the people in the village. She was also reportedly an excellent cook. She still owned some land but was unable to make a profit from it. As she told Mira in a letter three years after James's death, "the lands are mostly sold to the Canada Company [a British land development firm]. I have given up the idea of trying to do anything with mine." This might have been a reference to some land left her by her father.

In 1844, Laura's youngest, Hannah Cartwright Secord, lost her husband, Hawley Williams, and she and her two girls, three-year-old Catherine Emma and one-year-old Caroline, came to live with Laura. Sadly, little Caroline died at the age of five.

Hannah was married again on March 17, 1847, this time to British-born Edward Pyke Carthew of Guelph. The couple lived together in Guelph for another thirty years and had five children between 1848 and 1856. Hannah Cartwright Secord Williams Carthew died in 1877, at the age of sixty.

Seven years after Colonel James FitzGibbon wrote the last of the three certificates on behalf of the Secords, one member of their family had an opportunity to show his support for this trusted friend of James and Laura.

FitzGibbon, who was Clerk of the Legislative Council of the Province of Canada at the time, was trying to get some financial reward for his past services rendered.

Acknowledging FitzGibbon's ability to quell riots, the government had sent him wherever they needed someone to perform in this capacity. He'd already had an encounter with the firebrand William Lyon Mackenzie during a noisy confrontation between two opposing political groups in Toronto. Mackenzie had tried to goad FitzGibbon into calling out the militia on that occasion. Instead, as FitzGibbon described it, "I then conducted Mackenzie to his house and shut him in, having at the door to use force, he was endeavouring to address the multitude which I would not permit." If anyone could keep Mackenzie quiet, it was FitzGibbon.

The government had ignored FitzGibbon's warning that Mackenzie's rebels were a very real threat to Toronto. When the rebels marched en masse down Yonge Street in December 1837, FitzGibbon had led the militia in an effective counterattack.

In recognition, the government decided to award him a grant of five thousand acres of land. The bill failed to receive the Crown's approval on technical grounds, and the government instead proposed an award of £1,000.

When the bill came up for discussion in the House of the Assembly, one member, Mr. Aylwin from Quebec, objected because, in his opinion, at Beaver Dams FitzGibbon "had monopolized honor which did not rightfully belong to him." Nevertheless, the bill to award FitzGibbon the money was passed.

Mr. Aylwin's objection bothered Charles Secord, Laura's son, and he wrote a letter in support of FitzGibbon to the editor of a religious publication called *The Church*, published in Cobourg, Ontario. The story ran in an issue of the publication in April 1845.

As proof that what he wrote was true, Charles included FitzGibbon's 1837 certificate that had been written for his mother:

To the Editor of the "Church'
Queenston, 11th April 1845

Now I think it proper that Mr. Aylwin should
be informed and that the country in general
should know in what way Col. FitzGibbon
achieved so much honor for the affair at Beaver
Dam. My mother, living on the frontier the
whole of the late American war, a warm supporter of the British cause, frequently met with
the American officers and upon the occasion
of the capture of the American troops at the
Beaver Dam, after our troops, consisting of a
small detachment under Col. FitzGibbon, the
Lieut. FitzGibbon of the 49th Regiment, and
some Indians, had taken up their position at
that place, overheard an American officer say
to another of the officers that they intended to
surprise and capture the British troops at the
Beaver Dam. Without waiting for further information my mother, a lone woman, at once left
her house to apprise the British troops of what
she had heard, and travelled on foot the whole
of the way, passing all of the American guards
and many of the Indian scouts who were placed
along the road, until she arrived at the Beaver
Dam, and enquiring for the officer in command
was introduced to Col. FitzGibbon … she then
told him what she had come for, and all she had
heard — that the Americans intended to make
an attack upon them and would no doubt, from

their superior numbers, capture them all. Col. FitzGibbon in consequence of this information prepared himself to meet the enemy, and soon after the attack being made the American troops were captured and one or two field-pieces taken — as the Colonel's certificate of my mother's services on that occasion, accompanying this communication, will shew. It might perhaps be as well for me while upon this subject further to state that I never heard my mother speak of ... any other officer being at the Beaver Dam at the time. Col. FitzGibbon was the only officer who appeared to be in command, to whom my mother gave the information, and who acted the part he so nobly did on that occasion.

I am, Sir, your most obedient servant,
Chas. B. Secord

Charles Secord's letter, although not intended to be about Laura but in support of FitzGibbon's right to a pension, became the first published account of the heroic walk Laura Secord had taken thirty-two years earlier. Now her secret had been made public.

16

The Prince's Gift

It appears that the public paid little notice to Charles Secord's 1845 letter to the editor of the religious magazine, *The Church,* but eight years later someone else felt Laura's story worthy of more attention. The June 1813 action at Beaver Dams was included in a series of articles written about the War of 1812 by author Gilbert Auchinleck. Laura's story, which she'd written herself at Auchinleck's request, ran in the *Anglo-American* magazine, Volume III, in November 1853. The series would later be published as a book titled *The War of 1812,* published in Toronto by Chewlett in 1862.

But it was in 1860 that an event occurred that would finally bring to the public's attention the name of Laura Secord, Canadian heroine.

In 1860, Albert Edward, the nineteen-year-old Prince of Wales and future King Edward VII, eldest son of Queen Victoria, toured British North America. He began the tour on July 23 in

His Royal Highness Albert Edward, Prince of Wales, at the age of nineteen, the year he visited Canada. From a photograph by John Watkins, Illustrated London News, *July 28, 1860.*

St. John's, Newfoundland, and travelling by ship and train continued westward. One of the items on the royal agenda while the prince was in Canada was to pay special homage to the loyal veterans of the War of 1812 and the 1837 Rebellion.

He'd been in the country for a month, and after touring the western part of the province of Canada, the royal train stopped at Fort Erie. Here the prince boarded the steamer *Clifton* for a trip down the Niagara River to Chippawa.

At eighty-five, Laura Secord was still mentally sharp and physically spry enough to want to be part of the crowd eagerly awaiting the arrival of the prince's ship at the dock in Chippawa. Besides, she had her own agenda: She was hoping to meet him in person and to give him a document she had written.

Laura's daughter Charlotte, who was then fifty-eight, accompanied her mother down to the waterfront. When the prince left the ship, stepping out onto a red carpet, he was greeted by a cheering throng that broke into "God Save the Queen."

Later, after a carriage ride that was part of a torch-lit procession, the prince arrived at the Pavilion Hotel on the Drummond Hill (Niagara Falls) common where he was scheduled to speak. Overnight he stayed at the estate of the late Sam Zimmerman, a wealthy contractor of such important projects as the second Welland Canal and the railroad from Hamilton to Niagara Falls. The Zimmerman mansion, with a view of the falls from its upstairs windows, had been decorated and furnished especially for the royal visitor.

In honour of the prince's visit, the falls were illuminated for the first time that night, lit by Bengal lights, the kind of warning lights used by ships at sea. These were combined with rockets and other fireworks to create a dazzling display. During his stay the prince was also treated to a special performance by the famous French tightrope walker Blondin, who made two crossings of the rapids above the falls — once carrying a man on his back and again while walking on stilts.

Laura had prepared a memorial for the Prince of Wales and would have liked to have been able to present it to him herself. Earlier, she had properly filed the document with the governor general, and Laura was confident that when the prince knew of her circumstances he would understand her motive for writing it.

It was her wish, and she began her memorial by begging the prince's forgiveness for taking this liberty, that he let his mother know of the service she and James had performed for the British during the War of 1812. Stressing her loyalty, she asked if he would tell the queen "the name of one who in the hour of trial and danger ... stood ever ready and willing to defend this country against every invasion come what might."

She attached to her memorial FitzGibbon's 1837 certificate describing the walk to De Cew's, and she added a statement written by Welland County Warden James Cummings, her neighbour. It read: "I certify that I have for many years, been personally acquainted with Mrs. Secord named in the above certificate; and that she is the person she represents herself to be in her memorial heretofore annexed. And further she is a person of the utmost respectable character."

On September 16, 1860, the prince attended services at the Church of the Holy Trinity in Chippawa. The Reverend William Leeming, who had conducted James's funeral, led the service. It is quite likely that Laura was, as usual, in her regular pew. Every Sunday morning she left her cottage, crossed the wooden bridge, and walked to the church on the other side of Chippawa Creek.

A number of parishioners were presented to the prince following the church service, although it is not known if Laura was one of them. Perhaps he instead called at her cottage. If she was *ever* able to present the prince with her memorial we cannot be sure. He did, however, on a different occasion, notice her signature — the only woman's signature on an address presented to him by the veterans of 1812.

The veterans had decided to present a signed address to the royal visitor, and they let it be known that anyone who wanted to sign it could do so ahead of time at the office of the Clerk of the Peace at Niagara-on-the-Lake.

Laura wanted her name to be included, and she made the trip and called in at the clerk's office.

She may have travelled to her destination on the train. By this time the railroad between Chippawa and Queenston had been rebuilt for steam and had been extended to Niagara-on-the-Lake.

At first the clerk refused to let her put the signature on the document, but Laura, as determined as ever, would not back down. She may well have seen the prince's visit as her last opportunity for some sort of belated recognition of her heroism.

She got some support for her position from the *Niagara Mail & Empire* which wrote, on August 8, 1860, "Laura Secord insisted, and rightly so, for she had done her country more signal service than half the soldiers and militiamen engaged in the war. We say the brave, loyal old lady not only be allowed to sign the address but she deserves a special introduction to the Prince as a worthy example of the fire of 1812 when both men and women vied alike in the resolution to defend the country."

Laura probably didn't get the special introduction to the prince, but when the veterans' address was given to his Royal Highness at a ceremony at Queenston Heights, someone pointed out her signature. Intrigued, the prince began asking questions about this woman and what her current situation might be.

The prince's visit to Queenston on September 18, where he paid homage to Sir Isaac Brock and the veterans, had been the most important item on the tour's agenda. If Laura had been present at the ceremony she would have seen how the crush of the crowd forced the prince to get out of the carriage and continue on foot to the platform.

After the speeches, the Prince of Wales laid a stone to mark the spot where Brock had fallen on October 13, 1812, and he was then escorted inside Brock's monument. Climbing the 235-step spiral staircase to the indoor platform, he looked out at the magnificent view of Lake Ontario to the north and Niagara Falls to the south.

As Laura had hoped he would, the royal visitor decided to do something to acknowledge her bravery. After he returned to England he discussed with the queen Laura's financial distress and learned the British government's position on providing civilian heroines some assistance.

Early in 1861 the Prince of Wales sent Laura a reward of £100 in gold. Some sources state that the gift was delivered to her at her Chippawa cottage by ten men who had been part of the prince's entourage. It was the only compensation she would ever receive for her part in the War of 1812.

It wasn't long before the press got wind of the prince's gift. In 1861 the *Niagara Mail* wrote, "The Prince of Wales is a true, gallant Prince, with a warm regard for old ladies as well as to the young ones."

Suddenly, the public was eager to know more about this heroic woman who had been living in their midst. The *Niagara Mail* continued to follow Laura's saga, reprinting an earlier article from the *Welland Reporter* that had told the whole story:

> During the war of 1812–13, Mrs. Secord who was quite a young woman at the time, was living on a farm about midway between Queenston and St. David's [*sic*], both of which places were at that period occupied by American troops. During their frequent visits at their house she overheard them planning a surprise and night attack upon a detachment of British soldiers stationed near the Beaverdams, under the command of Lieut. FitzGibbon. Without betraying any knowledge of the affair, this brave woman set off by night through the

woods, a distance of thirteen miles to the British camp notwithstanding the imminent peril of falling into the hands of the American scouts or hostile Indians, and gave the British commander such information as enabled him to successfully repel the attack and defeat the Americans with great slaughter.... Mrs. S. is now over eighty years of age, in possession of all her faculties and she yet takes much pleasure in recounting her adventures upon the occasion above alluded to. The gift of the Prince will doubtless afford much satisfaction, as well to the members of her family and other relatives as to her many friends by whom she is held in much esteem. We trust the old lady may long be spared to the unimpaired enjoyment of all the comforts of this life.

Although there were a number of errors in the text, this and future articles on the subject made the public aware of Laura Secord and her courageous walk. Finally, a generation after the event that made her so, Laura was famous.

Seven years later, on October 17, 1868, at the age of ninety-three, Laura Ingersoll Secord died quietly at her home in Chippawa. She was buried beside her beloved husband James in the Drummond Hill Cemetery. Her obituary in the *Niagara Mail*, besides getting Laura's age wrong, managed to exaggerate the facts of her heroic walk by stating that, "Mrs. Secord hastened on foot through dense forests, and in the night."

Laura's only unmarried daughter, Charlotte, stayed in Canada until after her mother's estate had been settled. The will included some special bequests, and the balance of the estate went to Charlotte and Harriet, the only two of Laura's daughters still living. Charles had already been given the Queenston house.

After selling the cottage in Chippawa, Charlotte, who had lived there and in Guelph, went to visit Ireland again. She never returned to Canada, and died in 1880 at the age of eighty-two. Harriet, who never remarried, and her daughters went to live in Guelph. She died there in June 1892. Four years after his mother's death, Charles Badeau died. He was sixty-three. None of Laura's children lived to reach the age their mother had.

17

The Heroine and the Controversy

Three years after Laura had received the gift from the prince, a book written by Canadian historian and government official William F. Coffin, *1812: The War and Its Moral: A Canadian Chronicle*, was published. In it the author rightly treated Laura Secord as a heroine, but he made one glaring mistake: he called her "Mary." He also added bits of fiction to her story, in order to make it more interesting.

According to Coffin's book, James Secord had been the one who heard the plans of the American attack when he was out and about, and he'd gone hobbling home to tell "Mary." When Mary/Laura left the house that fateful morning, en route to warn the British at Beaver Dams, Coffin wrote that she milked a cow, in order to prove to the American sentry that she was only on her way to get some milk. William Coffin was the first author to include what would become the now-famous cow in the story.

Apparently, the cow suited the image of the Secords' pioneer lifestyle, and it soon became part of the legend, adopted by later authors of historical novels.

Sometime in the 1860s, while Laura was still living, an American historian and artist, Benson J. Lossing, visited Canada, gathering firsthand accounts for a book he was writing — *The Pictorial Field Book of the War of 1812* (Harpers, New York, 1869).

Lossing interviewed a number of residents of the Niagara Peninsula and travelled around, sketching scenes where the various battles had taken place. It is unclear whether or not Lossing met personally with Laura; he may have corresponded with her. He asked her for a personal account of her walk to Beaver Dams and for a picture of herself. She sent him both; the daguerreotype photograph had been taken some years earlier by Mr. Joel Lyons of Chippawa.

The account she produced for Lossing was similar to the one she'd sent Gilbert Auchinleck in 1853. Since Laura was now in her late eighties and the handwriting on this document is different from her first account, it may have been written for her by her granddaughter, Laura Louisa Smith, who based it on Laura's 1853 account.

Lossing included part of Laura's letter in a footnote in his book. By this time, Laura was adding a few embellishments of her own to the story. Time has a way of changing memory. Or perhaps Laura Louisa is responsible. "I had much difficulty in getting through the American guards. They were ten miles out in the country." The first account had suggested that Laura had merely *thought* she might encounter this difficulty.

At last historians and writers were giving Laura Secord credit for the victory at Beaver Dams. And because she was a woman she held a unique place in Canadian history. Interestingly, the biographers usually played down the fact that the Ingersolls had been "late Loyalists," forgetting to mention that Laura's father had fought in the American War of Independence *against* the British.

Even the respected historian Colonel E.A. Cruikshank enhanced the myth of the cow by hooking a milk pail over Laura's arm as she leaves the house. Other later writers made her out to be so naive as to set out on her walk barefoot; another fancied her wearing "stockings with red clocks on the side and a pair of low shoes with buckles."

In 1887, Sarah Anne Curzon, a British-born writer living in Toronto, published a drama in blank verse titled *Laura Secord, the Heroine of 1812*. An activist for women's suffrage, Curzon was the co-founder in 1885 of the Women's Canadian Historical Society of Toronto, along with Mary Agnes FitzGibbon, the granddaughter of Colonel James FitzGibbon.

Sarah Anne Curzon included both the cow and the milk pail in the story of Laura's walk, and she further embellished the tale by having Laura faint dramatically as soon as she delivers her message to FitzGibbon.

Laura's grandson, James Badeau Secord (1836–1899) of Niagara, the second son of Charles, wrote a letter in 1887 at Sarah Curzon's request in which he described how humble Laura had been whenever she spoke within the family circle about her courageous deed. "My grandmother was of modest disposition, and did not care to have her exploit mentioned, as she did not think she had done anything extraordinary. She was the very last one to mention the affair, and unless asked would never say anything about it."

Curzon also wrote a short, prose biography, *The Story of Laura Secord, 1813*, which was published in 1891 with the support of the Lundy's Lane Historical Society. She dramatized the scene where Laura emerges from the woods into the clearing where the Indians are camped by writing that the chief "threw up his tomahawk to strike her."

It was Laura's third daughter, Harriet, who remembered her mother leaving the house at dawn the day of her walk to warn FitzGibbon, and from her we get the description of Laura's clothing that Curzon included in her biography: "She had on house slippers and a flowered, print gown; I think it was brown, with orange flowers; at least a yellow tint is connected in my mind with that particular morning."

Sarah Anne Curzon's purpose in writing the biography was to raise funds for a memorial stone to be placed on Laura's grave in the Drummond Hill Cemetery. She ended her memoir of Laura with these words, written at Toronto, August 4, 1887:

> But surely we who enjoy happiness she so largely secured for us, we who have known how to honour Brock and Brant, will also know how to honour Tecumseh and Laura Secord; the heroine as well as the heroes of our Province — of our Common Dominion — and will no longer delay to do it, lest Time should snatch the happy opportunity from us.

A competition had been held for the design of the monument, and it was won by painter and sculptor Mildred Peel. Unveiled on June 22, 1901, the eight-foot-high monument featured a bronze bust of Laura as a young woman, set on a granite pedestal. It replaced the two marble slabs originally on the Secords' graves that were later transferred to the Church of the Holy Trinity in Chippawa. Unfortunately, Sarah Anne Curzon died in 1898 and never saw the finished monument.

*Bust of Laura Secord by Mildred Peel, O.S.A. From
the collection of the Archives of Ontario.*

Another biography, *The Story of Laura Secord and Canadian
Reminiscences,* appeared in 1900, written by Emma A. Currie,
who had lived all her life in the Niagara Peninsula and who was
the founder in 1892 of the St. Catharines Literary Club. Currie
had interviewed members of both the Ingersoll and Secord families for the book, and she wrote a straightforward account of
Laura's life, avoiding any exaggerations.

It was Laura's great-niece, Elizabeth Ann Gregory, a granddaughter of Stephen Secord's widow Hannah, who told Currie

there had been no cow in the story. "The cow and the milk pail are a fable," she said.

The royalties from Currie's book were to go toward the erection of a monument of Laura at Queenston Heights. Currie had hoped for a say in the design of the monument and had a sketch drawn up of David Secord's great-granddaughter, dressed in the clothes Laura is supposed to have worn for her walk. The girl was said to have looked very much like the young Laura Secord. The sketch was politely rejected, however, and today the medallion on the monument shows Laura as an elderly woman, not as she was at the time of her heroic walk.

One man had come on foot twenty miles in order to make a donation toward the monument, saying he had fond memories of Laura. He told Emma Currie that when he was a boy at Chippawa, his family was very poor. He used to shovel snow for Laura, he said, and she always saw to it that he had a hot breakfast when he was finished. Laura had also knit for him the first pair of mitts he ever owned.

Laura's granddaughter, Alicia Cockburn (daughter of Charles) provided Currie with a personal description of Laura: "… kind, brown eyes, a sweet loving smile hovering about her mouth. This did not denote weakness. She was about five feet four inches tall and slight in form."

Erected by the government of Canada, which had provided a grant to supplement the donations and Currie's royalties, the monument to Laura Secord at Queenston Heights was unveiled July 15, 1911. There was a huge crowd at the ceremony, including about three thousand Canadians, some visitors from the United States, and several of Laura's descendants. The twelve-foot-high, grey granite pedestal was located not far from Brock's Monument. It seems ironic that the woman who had been denied by the government the opportunity of looking after Brock's Monument now had a one of her own in the same park at Queenston Heights.

Laura's monument is set apart in an attractive area of its own, surrounded by neatly trimmed hedges, paving stones, and a low, wrought iron fence. From the stone wall behind the monument, today's visitor to the park looks down over the escarpment to the town of Queenston and out at the winding Niagara River as it makes its way to Lake Ontario.

Laura Secord monument at Queenston Heights.

—*//*—

In the 1920s, after a number of biographies had been written about her, monuments and markers unveiled, poetry and drama written about her walk, even her portrait painted and hung in Toronto's parliament buildings in 1905, Laura Secord was at the peak of her popularity.

But in the 1930s some skeptics began to question whether or not she could rightly be called a heroine.

The controversy began with the publication of two books by historian and author William Stewart Wallace, then librarian at the University of Toronto. His first book, *A History of the Canadian People*, was authorized in 1930 by the Ontario Ministry of Education for use in the schools. Conspicuous by its absence in the chapter on the War of 1812 was any mention of Laura Secord.

The *Toronto Star* brought the subject to light in a front page article that ran on December 1, 1931. It was a report of an interview with Wallace, in which he had voiced the opinion that Laura's walk had had no historical significance. He believed Colonel FitzGibbon had been warned of the impending American attack by his Native scouts, even before Laura arrived at Beaver Dams. He went so far as to suggest that James and Laura Secord had fabricated the entire story, in order to add weight to their post-war petitions to the government for some form of compensation. This heresy sparked a war of words in the press.

Immediately, all four of Toronto's papers were flooded with letters of protest. How dare William Stewart Wallace!

Henry Cartwright Secord, a descendant of James's brother Stephen, was determined to set the record straight. He wrote to the *Mail and Empire*, quoting sources that included FitzGibbon's 1837 certificate that proved Wallace was wrong.

Wallace stood firm, and in a letter to the *Mail and Empire* on December 30, 1931, he wrote, "As for the idea that Laura Secord 'saved the situation' at Beaver Dams it is too absurd for serious discussion … and I venture to believe that any competent historical scholar who examines the evidence will be forced to pronounce it a myth."

His own examination of the evidence was about to be called into question.

Early in 1932, Wallace produced a small book in support of his argument called *The Story of Laura Secord: A Study in Historical Evidence*. In it Wallace pointed out the fact that FitzGibbon had said nothing about Laura Secord in his official reports on the Battle at Beaver Dams on June 24, 1813. And furthermore, how reliable could FitzGibbon's testimony of 1837 be when he admitted that he'd written it "in a Moment of much hurry and from Memory"?

Wallace accepted the fact that Laura had walked to FitzGibbon's headquarters, but he insisted that the walk had been in vain. Certainly she'd shown courage and patriotism, but the information she'd delivered had played no part in the victory at Beaver Dams.

What were the supporters of Laura Secord to believe? The editor of the *Globe* stated, "There can be no doubt she performed the journey for the deliberate purpose of warning the British and that she remains a great Canadian heroine." But was that enough?

It was Henry Cartwright Secord who discovered in 1934, in the Public Archives of Canada in Ottawa, the earliest certificate written for Laura Secord by FitzGibbon in 1820, a mere seven years after the Battle of Beaver Dams. It had been written in support of James Secord's request to occupy part of the military reserve at Queenston for a stone quarry. Parts of that certificate have been previously quoted here.

The Niagara Historical Society had already published the certificate ten years before this, in a paper written by Janet Carnochan, the well-respected historian of the Niagara area, but until Henry Secord found it for a *second* time, it hadn't been given much publicity.

Henry Secord sent a copy of it to Fred Williams, columnist at the *Mail and Empire*. On June 23, 1934, the paper published Secord's covering letter and the certificate. For the first time the certificate became public knowledge.

This 1820 document said much the same as had the one written in 1837, but since it had been penned years earlier, it confirmed that the evidence of the 1837 certificate was true, and also that there had been nothing wrong with FitzGibbon's memory.

One thing it did include was the statement that the attack had come the morning of the second day after Laura had given FitzGibbon her information. The attack had come on June 24, therefore Laura must have made her walk on June 22, not the 23rd as everyone had previously thought.

But had Laura's walk still been in vain?

In the appendix of a book by William Perkins Bull, titled *From Brock to Currie* (1935), the author presented "Documents Regarding Laura Secord's Trip to Beaver Dams," evidence he'd compiled that led to the opposite conclusion to that of Wallace.

Although he never admitted he'd been wrong (somehow in his research he'd failed to find the 1820 certificate in the public archives), Wallace may have backed off a little. In 1935–37, as the editor of the *Encyclopedia of Canada*, in the article on Laura

Secord, he described her as a heroine, but stayed clear of mentioning the date of her arrival at Beaver Dams and whether the message she'd delivered to FitzGibbon had been of any use to the British.

He wrote, "In the summer of 1813, while American troops were billeted in her house in Queenston, she came into possession of knowledge of the American plans for a surprise attack on Beaver Dams; she made her way through American lines, and warned Lieut. James FitzGibbon, in command at Beaver Dams, of the projected attack." Period.

It is unfortunate that earlier embellishments to the truth — the cow, the milk pail, the trek through the woods at night, on bare feet, made serious historians suspicious of Laura's story. But she would yet be vindicated.

In 1959, a third certificate written for Laura by FitzGibbon was discovered, again in the Public Archives of Canada in Ottawa. Written at York, May 11, 1827, this was FitzGibbon's second and most important certificate because in it he stated clearly that Laura reached De Cew's after sunset on June 22, even before the Americans had left Fort George. Although Laura had believed the attack would come the next day, FitzGibbon, "in consequence of this information," had time to get the Natives and his own men into position to intercept the attack when it did come. There was no doubt that Laura had delivered the information, but now there could also be no doubt about the fact that she'd gone a day earlier than previously thought. Clearly then, hers was the first warning.

When the attack didn't come the next morning, Ducharme and his Native warriors went on a scouting expedition and saw American soldiers crossing the Niagara River at Fort George. Because the attack was expected, the Indian scouts went out early on the morning of the 24th, returning with the news that the Americans were approaching.

These scouting expeditions were made *because* of Laura's warning.

Each of FitzGibbon's three certificates had been written at Laura's request to support her petitions, although the reason for the one is 1837 is unknown. It was used for the first time in 1840 when Laura was asking to be given the ferry concession at Queenston.

It appears that Laura had sent the original certificates with her petitions, without making a copy for herself, and these originals became buried in the government's files. She did make copies of the 1837 certificate, however, because she was able to provide one whenever she needed some proof of her walk to Beaver Dams, as she did for Gilbert Auchinleck for *Anglo-American* magazine. This, then, became the best-known certificate, but it was the discovery of the 1827 document that finally settled the controversy over Laura's rightful place in the annals of Canadian history.

Epilogue

In Toronto in 1913, Frank O'Connor, a man who would be named to the Canadian senate in 1935, began a small candy company on Yonge Street, selling handmade chocolates. He wanted to give his chocolates a name that signified wholesomeness and purity, something of a Canadian tradition, and he chose the name of a Canadian icon, Laura Secord. Before long, little white cottage-style Laura Secord candy shops began to spring up across the country.

The candy company was sold to Ault Foods (John Labatt Limited) of London, Ontario, in 1969, and shortly thereafter that company purchased the house in Queenston where James and Laura Secord had lived from 1803 to 1835. The house was renovated, restored, and furnished with original period furniture, and in 1998 it was donated to the Niagara Parks Commission, which maintains it as a tourist attraction.

In 1905, the Women's Literary Club had laid a stone marker in front of the house, marking the spot where Laura's famous walk began.

Back in 1931, the Niagara Parks Commission had considered buying Laura's cottage at 3800 Bridgewater Street in Chippawa where she'd lived for twenty-seven years. On further inspection, however, it was determined that it needed too much work to make it feasible. Today, it is an attractive private residence.

For some years now there has been a library on the site of Thomas Ingersoll's home on Main Street in Great Barrington, Massachusetts, the place where Laura was born and where she spent her first twenty years. Interestingly, the Ingersolls' frame house was still there as late as 1913 when the library was built.

On October 18, 1997, on a day they designated as "Laura Secord Day," the Great Barrington Historic District Commission dedicated a plaque in front of the Mason Library, a tribute to a heroine on the other side of the War of 1812.

The plaque reads:

> Laura Ingersoll was born in a dwelling which stood on this site till 1913 when Mason Library was built. She was the daughter of Elizabeth (Dewey) and Thomas Ingersoll, a hatter and a miller with privilege nearby on the Housatonic River. Looking for new opportunity the Ingersolls relocated to Upper Canada in 1795. Laura married James Secord, a United Empire Loyalist. They were living in Queenston, Ontario at the outbreak of the War of 1812. Alerted to an impending American attack at Beaver Dams, Laura Secord in June 1813 undertook an arduous

19 mile journey through woods and swamp to
warn British troops. Her tenacity and courage
made her a heroine. Laura Secord was honored
on a Canadian postage stamp in 1992.

The stamp to which the plaque refers was issued by Canada Post.
It depicts a youthful Laura — she was only thirty-seven at the
time — hurrying through the woods, and it includes in the lower
right corner three small silhouettes, representing the Native warriors who played such a large part in the victory at Beaver Dams.

At Beaver Dams Battlefield Park there is another plaque
that reads, "Laura Ingersoll Secord, 1775–1868 who set out from
home in Queenston early in the morning of June 22, 1813, to
walk an arduous nineteen miles to warn the British outpost at
DeCew Falls of an impending American attack. The information
enabled the local commander, Lieutenant James FitzGibbon, and
his detachment to surprise and capture the entire enemy force at
the Battle of Beaver Dams on June 24, 1813, thereby marking the
turning point in the War of 1812. To perpetuate her memory."

Just how significant was the British victory at Beaver Dams?
It would be an exaggeration to say that Laura Secord saved
Canada. The Battle of Beaver Dams was only one link in a chain
of events that would eventually bring an end to the War of 1812.
But it was important because it gave the British the advantage
in the Niagara Peninsula. It ended the American occupation of
Queenston and area in 1813, in the middle of the summer, the
best season to move an army about, and it prevented the enemy
from any further advancement that year.

On November 5, 2006, the governor general of Canada,
Michaëlle Jean, dedicated the life-sized statues of fourteen
Canadians — men and woman of remarkable courage — at the

Valiants Memorial, near the National War Memorial in Ottawa. Among the fourteen statues, there are only two women. One of them is Laura Secord.

Statue of Laura Secord at Valiants Memorial, Ottawa, Ontario.

Chronology of Laura Secord

Laura and Her Times	Canada and the World
1629	**1629**
Richard Ingersoll, the first member of the Ingersoll family to come to British North America, arrives at Salem, Massachusetts, from Bedfordshire, England.	July 20. Samuel de Champlain, creator of New France, surrenders Quebec to English adventurer David Kirke and his brothers. Champlain is captured and taken to England. The English will occupy Quebec until 1632.
1749	**1749**
Birth of Thomas Ingersoll, father of Laura Ingersoll Secord, at Westfield, Massachusetts.	The British found Halifax as a settlement and military base. The town will replace Annapolis Royal as the capital of Nova Scotia.
1758	**1758**
January 28. Birth of Elizabeth	The French surrender Fortress

Laura and Her Times

(Betsy) Dewey, mother of Laura Ingersoll, at Westfield, Massachusetts.

1773
Birth of James Secord, future husband of Laura Ingersoll, at New Rochelle, New York.

1775
February 28. Thomas Ingersoll marries Elizabeth Dewey in Great Barrington, Massachusetts.

September 13. Birth of Laura, first child of Thomas and Elizabeth Ingersoll, at Great Barrington, Massachusetts.

1779
October 17. Birth of Elizabeth Franks, second daughter of Thomas and Elizabeth Ingersoll.

1781
Birth of Mira (Myra), third daughter of Thomas and Elizabeth Ingersoll.

Canada and the World

Louisbourg, in the far corner of Île Royale (Cape Breton Island), to the English for the last time.

1773
The Boston Tea Party, a protest by the Americans against British taxation, takes place in Boston Harbor.

1775
Quebec, Nova Scotia, and Prince Edward Island decide not to join the Thirteen Colonies in the American Revolution to gain independence from British rule.

1776
July 4. The U.S. Congress signs the Declaration of Independence.

1779
Governor Frederick Haldimand establishes a subscription library at Quebec City, the first of its kind in Canada.

1781
October. British general Lord Cornwallis surrenders to the Americans at Yorkton, Virginia, after a siege by American and French troops led by General George Washington. It is the last

Laura and Her Times

Canada and the World

battle of the Revolutionary War.

1783
Birth of Abigail, fourth daughter of Thomas and Elizabeth Ingersoll.

1783
The Treaty of Paris ends the American War of Independence between the United States and Great Britain.

1784
February 20. Death of Elizabeth (Betsy) Dewey, mother of Laura Ingersoll and her three younger sisters.

1784
August 16. A new province is formed when Britain divides Nova Scotia at the Chignecto Isthmus, naming the west and north portion "New Brunswick."

1785
May 26. Widower Thomas Ingersoll marries his second wife, Mercy Smith.

1785
Sixteen-year-old Isaac Brock joins Britain's 49th Infantry Regiment as a junior officer.

1789
Mercy Smith Ingersoll, second wife of Thomas Ingersoll, dies. Thomas Ingersoll marries Sarah (Sally) Backus, his third wife.

1789
George Washington becomes the first president of the United States.

1791
September 27. Birth of Charles Fortescue, son of Thomas Ingersoll and Sally Backus, and first half-brother for Laura Ingersoll, at Great Barrington, Massachusetts.

1791
The *Constitutional Act* divides the old colony of Quebec into Upper and Lower Canada, two distinct provinces, each with its own elected assembly and appointed upper house.

1793
Thomas Ingersoll and associates petition Lieutenant-Governor

1793
July 7. Lieutenant-Governor John Graves Simcoe passes the

Laura and Her Times

Simcoe for a grant of land in Upper Canada.

1795
Thomas Ingersoll and family move from Massachusetts to Upper Canada. Thomas operates a tavern in Queenston while he clears the land for his settlement at Oxford-on-the-Thames.

1796
The Ingersoll family moves into the log house in Oxford-on-the-Thames after the survey of the township is completed.

1797
Laura Ingersoll marries James Secord and the couple takes up residence in St. Davids.

1799
Laura and James Secord's first child, Mary, is born in St. Davids.

Canada and the World

Act Against Slavery, prohibiting the importation of slaves into Upper Canada.

1794
Britain signs the Jay Treaty with the United States, agreeing to withdraw from the American side of the border before June 1, 1796.

1795
Birth in Dundee, Scotland, of William Lyon Mackenzie, who will become a controversial figure in the political life of Upper Canada and the first mayor of Toronto.

1796
February 1. York (Toronto) becomes the capital of Upper Canada, replacing Newark (Niagara-on-the-Lake).

1797
The Americans launch their first lake schooner, the *Washington*, on Lake Erie, near Presque Isle.

1799
The Danforth Road, intended to connect Toronto with the Trent River at the Bay of Quinte, is completed as far as Hope Township, a total of sixty miles (ninety-six kilometres).

Laura and Her Times

1801
Laura and James Secord's second daughter, Charlotte, is born in St. Davids.

1803
Laura and James Secord's third daughter, Harriet, is born in St. Davids.

The Secords move to their new house in Queenston.

1805
Thomas Ingersoll and family abandon the settlement of Oxford-on-the-Thames and move to the Credit River.

1809
Birth of a son for James and Laura Secord, Charles Badeau, at Queenston.

1810
Birth at Queenston of Appolonia (Appy), fourth daughter for James and Laura Secord.

1812
Thomas Ingersoll, father of Laura Ingersoll Secord, dies at Port Credit.

Canada and the World

1801
Great Britain and Ireland merge to form the United Kingdom of Great Britain and Ireland.

1803
The United States doubles in size with the purchase of the Louisiana Territory from France — more than two million square kilometres, at a cost of $15 million.

1805
The Battle of Trafalgar eliminates the French and Spanish naval fleets, giving Britain command of the sea.

1809
March 30. The *Labrador Act* gives Labrador to Newfoundland.

1810
September 12. Death at Montreal of Joseph Frobisher, fur trader and merchant who, along with his brother Benjamin and others, had been part of the North West Company.

1812
June 16. The United States declares war on Great Britain. The War of 1812 begins.

Laura and Her Times

October 13. James Secord is seriously wounded at the Battle of Queenston Heights.

1813

James and Laura Secord and family return to Queenston, after spending the winter at St. Davids, where James was convalescing.

June 21. Laura overhears the American plan to attack the British outpost at Beaver Dams.

June 22. Laura leaves home before daylight to warn Lieutenant James FitzGibbon, arriving at his headquarters at De Cew's house after dark that same night.

June 24. Laura returns home when the Battle of Beaver Dams ends with the surrender of the American forces.

Canada and the World

July 12. American brigadier general Hull invades Upper Canada at Sandwich, above Fort Amherstburg.

August 16. Brock's forces and Tecumseh, with his Native troops, capture Detroit.

October 13. Major General Isaac Brock is killed at the Battle of Queenston Heights.

1813

April 27. American troops under Major General Dearborn capture York.

May 27. Americans capture Fort George, and the British under General John Vincent retreat to Burlington Heights.

June 6. The Battle of Stoney Creek.

June 23. Americans under Lieutenant Colonel Charles Boerstler leave Fort George for Beaver Dams, first camping overnight at Queenston.

June 24. Americans surrender to Lieutenant James FitzGibbon, after being ambushed in the beech woods by Native troops.

September 10. The Battle of

Laura and Her Times

Canada and the World

Lake Erie. American commander Oliver Perry is victorious over British commander Robert Barclay.

October 5. The British are defeated at the Battle of the Thames at Moraviantown, and Shawnee chief Tecumseh is killed.

October 25. The Battle of Châteauguay in Lower Canada is an all-Canadian victory.

November 11. American troops are out-manoeuvred at the Battle of Crysler's Farm.

December 10. Brigadier General George McClure's American forces burn the town of Newark before retreating to Fort Niagara.

December 19. After capturing Fort Niagara, the British burn Lewiston, New York.

December 29. The British forces burn Buffalo.

1814
March 31. The War in Europe ends when the allies capture Paris and Napoleon gives up.

July 3. The British garrison at Fort Erie surrenders to the

Laura and Her Times

Canada and the World

Americans, led by Major General Jacob Brown.

July 5. The Battle of Chippawa, which leads to re-occupation of Queenston by the Americans.

July 19. Americans under Colonel Isaac Stone burn the Loyalist village of St. Davids.

July 25. The Battle of Lundy's Lane, the bloodiest battle of the War of 1812.

August 21–25. British forces capture Washington and burn the White House and several public buildings.

September 21. General Drummond abandons the siege against the Americans at Fort Erie.

November 1. The Americans withdraw across the river, blowing up Fort Erie.

December 24. The Treaty of Ghent is signed, ending the War of 1812.

1815
January 8. The Battle of New Orleans is a victory for the Americans, but the war is already over.

Laura and Her Times

1816
April 18. Mary Secord, eldest daughter of James and Laura, marries Dr. William Trumbull at Niagara Falls.

Charles Ingersoll, half-brother of Laura Secord, marries Anna Maria Merritt.

1817
March 27. Birth of the first grandchild of James and Laura Secord, Elizabeth Trumbull, daughter of Mary Secord and Dr. William Trumbull, in Ireland.

Charles Ingersoll buys his (and Laura's) father's old farm at Oxford-on-the-Thames. He and his brother James establish a new village there called "Ingersoll."

Birth of seventh and last child of James and Laura Secord, Hannah Cartwright, in Queenston.

1820
James Secord petitions the government for a licence to operate a stone quarry on the military reserve at Queenston.

Canada and the World

1816
June 19. The Seven Oaks Massacre, the destruction of the Hudson's Bay Company's Red River settlement by agents of the rival North West Company, leads to a merger of the two.

1817
Construction begins on the Lachine Canal to bypass the rapids in the St. Lawrence River, upstream from Montreal.

The Rush-Bagot Agreement is signed, limiting the size of the U.S. and British forces on the Great Lakes.

1820
January 29. Death at the age of eighty-two of King George III, the British monarch at the time of the American Revolution. He had suffered bouts of mental illness, possibly due to the hereditary blood disease porphyria.

Laura and Her Times

1824
November 23. Harriet Secord, daughter of James and Laura, marries St. Catharines lawyer, David William Smith.

1828
James Secord is appointed registrar of the Niagara District Surrogate Court.

December 20. The Secords' fourth daughter, Appolonia (Appy), dies of typhus at the age of eighteen.

1830
November 26. Charles Badeau Secord, only son of James and Laura, marries Margaret Ann Robins of Kingston.

1832
Laura's half-brother, Charles Ingersoll, dies in the cholera epidemic at the age of forty-one.

1833
April 22. The Secords' youngest daughter, Hannah, marries Hawley Williams, a settler from Guelph.

May 9. James and Laura's first grandson is born, Charles Forsyth Secord, son of Charles and Margaret Ann.

Canada and the World

1824
William Lyon Mackenzie opens a newspaper office in Queenston, publishing the *Colonial Advocate*.

1828
November 3. Sir John Colborne is appointed lieutenant-governor of Upper Canada.

1830
William Lyon Mackenzie is re-elected to the House of the Assembly as a Reformer, representing the County of York.

1832
A widespread cholera epidemic, the first to reach Canada, kills 10 percent of the population.

1833
Hamilton, Ontario, is incorporated as a city.

The *Slavery Abolition Act* bans slavery throughout the British Empire.

June 26. Captain John Ross and nineteen crew members

Laura and Her Times

James Secord is promoted to judge of the Niagara District Surrogate Court, and son Charles takes over his former position as registrar.

October 17. The Secords' daughter Laura Ann marries Captain John Poore.

1835
James Secord becomes Collector of His Majesty's Customs at the Port of Chippawa, and he and Laura move to the Customs House in the village.

1837
Captain John Poore, husband of Laura Ann Secord and father of John Jr., dies.

1840
Laura Secord petitions the lieutenant-governor for the ferry concession at Queenston. The petition is denied.

1841
February 22. James Secord dies at Chippawa as the result of a stroke, in his sixty-eighth year.

Canada and the World

are rescued from Baffin Island after being ice-bound for three months.

The Welland Canal from Port Dalhousie on Lake Ontario, to Port Robinson, to Port Colborne on Lake Erie opens.

1835
John A. MacDonald starts practising law in Kingston, Ontario.

Francis Bond Head is appointed lieutenant-governor of Upper Canada.

1837
In an attempt to overthrow the colonial government, William Lyon Mackenzie's men march down Yonge Street toward Toronto, but government Loyalists disperse them with a few shots.

1840
Brock's Monument is seriously damaged by an explosion set by Mackenzie supporter Benjamin Lett.

1841
February 10. The *Act of Union*, voted in the British parliament the year before, comes into effect,

Laura and Her Times

November. Newly widowed Laura Secord buys a cottage on the banks of Chippawa Creek. It will be her final home.

1842
May. Lawyer David William Smith, the husband of Harriet Secord, dies. Harriet and daughters Laura Louisa and Mary Augusta move in with Laura. Harriet's son William goes to live in Fort Erie where he will be raised by his father's parents.

1843
Laura's daughter Laura Ann marries her second husband, Dr. William Clarke of Guelph.

1844
Hannah Secord's husband, Hawley Williams, dies. Hannah and daughters Catherine Emma and Caroline move in with Laura at the Chippawa cottage.

1845
A letter written by Laura's son, Charles Badeau Secord, and published in the religious magazine *The Church*, makes public for the first time the story of Laura's heroic walk.

Canada and the World

uniting Upper and Lower Canada into the Province of Canada.

1842
September 16. The first La Fontaine-Baldwin cabinet is formed in the Province of Canada. The partnership will lead to the development of responsible government across the country.

1843
The short stories *A Christmas Carol* by Charles Dickens, and *The Tell-Tale Heart* by Edgar Allan Poe are published.

1844
The first publicly-funded telegraph line in the world, between Baltimore and Washington, ushers in the age of the telegraph.

1845
When blight causes the potato crop in Ireland to fail, the Irish potato famine begins. One and a half million people die of starvation and disease.

Laura and Her Times

1847
Hannah Secord Williams marries her second husband, Edward Pyke Carthew of Guelph.

1853
November. The story of Laura's heroic walk to Beaver Dams, written by herself at author Gilbert Auchinleck's request, appears in a series of articles about the War of 1812 in *Anglo-American* magazine.

1861
Laura receives a gift of £100 in gold from the Prince of Wales for her loyalty to the Crown in June 1813.

1863
Historian William F. Coffin, in his book *1812: The War and Its Moral*, depicts Laura Secord as a heroine.

Canada and the World

1847
March 3. Birth in Edinburgh, Scotland, of Alexander Graham Bell — teacher, scientist, and inventor of the telephone.

1853
The first locomotive built in Canada, the Toronto, is completed at the Toronto Locomotive Works.

Canadian author Susanna Moodie publishes *Life in the Clearings Versus the Bush*.

1861
April 12. Lieutenant Henry S. Farley, a Southerner, fires a ten-inch mortar round into Union-held Fort Sumter in Charleston Bay, starting the American Civil War.

1863
Charles Francis Hall begins his search for Arctic explorer John Franklin, later finding graves of some of his crewmen on King William Island.

1867
July 1. The proclamation of the *British North America Act* creates the Dominion of Canada, consisting of Ontario, Quebec, New Brunswick, and Nova Scotia.

Laura and Her Times

1868
October 17. Laura Ingersoll Secord dies in Chippawa at the age of ninety-three.

1869
The story of Laura's walk appears as a footnote in Benson J. Lossing's book *The Pictorial Field Book of the War of 1812.*

1887
Sarah Anne Curzon publishes a drama titled *Laura Secord, the Heroine of 1812.*

1891
Under the auspices of the Lundy's Lane Historical Society, Sarah Anne Curzon writes a short biography, *The Story of Laura Secord, 1813.*

1900
The Story of Laura Secord and Canadian Reminiscences is written by Emma A. Currie, the royalties from the book going toward building a monument to Laura Secord at Queenston Heights.

1901
June 22. A monument to Laura Secord is unveiled on the site of

Canada and the World

1868
April 7. Thomas D'Arcy McGee, MP, and a Father of Confederation, is shot and killed by suspected Fenian, James Patrick Whalen.

1869
November 17. The Suez Canal, linking the Mediterranean to the Red Sea, opens to navigation.

1887
The world's first electric streetcar system is inaugurated at St. Catharines, Ontario.

1891
Sir John A. MacDonald, the first Father of Confederation, dies.

1900
Canada sends a second contingent of volunteer soldiers to the Boer War in South Africa, where descendents of the Dutch fight for independence from Britain.

1901
January 22. Death of Queen Victoria, who had reigned Great

Laura and Her Times	*Canada and the World*
the graves of Laura and James at Drummond Hill Cemetery.	Britain for sixty-three years. Her eldest son, who had held the title Prince of Wales longer than any other heir apparent, becomes King Edward VII.

1911

July 15. A monument to Laura Secord is unveiled at Queenston Heights Park.

1911

May 31. RMS *Titanic* is launched at Belfast, Ireland.

Norwegian Roald Amundsen reaches the South Pole ahead of British Naval Officer Robert F. Scott.

1934

June 22. After Henry Cartwright Secord "discovers" FitzGibbon's 1820 certificate, written for Laura Secord, it is published in the *Niagara Mail and Empire,* the first time the certificate is made public.

1934

January 11. Birth of Jean Chrétien, Canada's twentieth prime minister, at Shawinigan, Quebec.

Adolph Hitler becomes the Führer of Germany.

1959

The discovery of FitzGibbon's 1827 certificate in the public archives settles the controversy over Laura's right to be called a Canadian heroine.

1959

A one-billion-dollar project, the St. Lawrence Seaway, opens after five years of construction.

1972

The Secords' Queenston house is restored and given to the Niagara Parks Commission to be maintained as a tourist attraction.

1972

January 30. Northern Ireland's Bloody Sunday. British soldiers shoot at Irish civil rights protesters, marching in Londonderry. Thirteen are killed.

Laura and Her Times

Canada and the World

1992
Canada Post issues a postage stamp commemorating Laura Secord.

1992
November 12. The Inuit endorse, by nearly 85 percent of voters, the creation of Nunavut, a semi-autonomous territory.

1997
The Great Barrington Historic District Commission dedicates a plaque on the site of the Ingersoll home in Great Barrington, Massachusetts.

1997
December 3. The Ottawa Convention or the Anti-Personnel Mine Ban Treaty that aims at eliminating landmines all over the world is signed.

2006
November 5. The life-sized statues of fourteen Canadian heroes and heroines, including Laura Secord, are dedicated at the Valiants Memorial in Ottawa.

2006
After being found guilty of crimes against humanity, the former president of Iraq, Saddam Hussein, is executed.

Bibliography

BOOKS

Bassett, John, and A. Roy Petrie. *Laura Secord*. Markham, ON: Fitzhenry & Whiteside Ltd., 2004.

Berton, Pierre. *Flames Across the Border: 1813–1814*. Toronto: McClelland and Stewart Ltd., 1981.

Bothwell, Robert. *A Short History of Ontario*. Edmonton: Hurtig Publishers Ltd., 1986.

Coates, Colin M., and Cecilia Morgan. *Heroines and History: Representations of Madeleine de Vercheres and Laura Secord*. Toronto: University of Toronto Press, 2002.

Crump, Jennifer. *The War of 1812 Against the States: Heroes of a Great Canadian Victory*. Canmore, AB: Altitude Publishing Canada Ltd., 2003.

Currie, Emma A. *The Story of Laura Secord and Canadian Reminiscences*. Toronto: William Briggs, 1900.

Gillman, Don, and Pierre Turgeon. *Canada, a People's History, Vol. I*. Toronto: McClelland and Stewart Ltd., 2000.

Graves, Dianne. *In The Midst of Alarms, The Untold Story of Women and the War of 1812*. Toronto: Robin Brass Studio Inc., 2007.

Hancock, Pat. *The Penguin Book of Canadian Biography for Young Readers: Early Canada*. Toronto: Penguin Books Canada Ltd., 1999.

Hemmings, David. *Laura Ingersoll Secord: A Heroine and Her Family*. Niagara-on-the-Lake, ON: Bygones Publishing, 2010.

Hume, Blanche. *Laura Secord*. 2nd ed. The Ryerson Canadian History Readers. Toronto: The Ryerson Press, 1935.

Lunn, Janet. *Laura Secord, A Story of Courage*. Toronto: Tundra Books, 2001.

MacDonald, Cheryl. *Laura Secord: The Heroic Adventures of a Canadian Legend*. Canmore, AB: Altitude Publishing Canada Ltd., 2005.

Mallory, Enid. *The Green Tiger, James FitzGibbon: A Hero of the War of 1812*. Toronto: McClelland and Stewart Ltd., 1976.

McKenzie, Ruth. *Laura Secord: The Legend and the Lady*. Toronto: McClelland and Stewart Ltd., 1971.

McLeod, Carol. *Legendary Canadian Women*. Hantsport, N.S.: Lancelot Press, 1983: 131–35.

Robinson, Helen Caister. *Laura: A Portrait of Laura Secord*. Toronto: Dundurn Press, 1981.

Russell, Loris. *Everyday Life in Colonial Canada*. London, UK: B.T. Batsford, 1973.

Smelser, Marshall. *American History at a Glance*. New York: Barnes and Noble, 1959.

Smith, Chard Powers. *The Housatonic: Puritan River*. New York: Rinehart, 1946.

Taylor, Charles J. *History of Great Barrington (Berkshire County) Massachusetts*. Great Barrington, MA: C.W. Bryan and Co., 1882.

Turner, Wesley B. *The War of 1812: The War That Both Sides Won*. Toronto: Dundurn Press, 1990.

ELECTRONIC DOCUMENTS

Arnt, Calvin. "A Concise History of Butler's Rangers." *www.butlersrangers.ca* (accessed October 15, 2011).

"Battle of Crysler's Farm." War of 1812–14. *war1812.tripod.com/batcrys.html* (accessed October 29, 2011).

Benn, Carl. "The Loyal and Patriotic Society." City of Toronto Museums and Heritage Services. *www.napoleon-series.org/military/*

Warof1812/2007/Issue6/c_benn.html (accessed October 17, 2011).

The BerkshireWeb. "Great Barrington Massachusetts." *www.berkshireweb.com/themap/greatbarrington/history/index.html* (accessed October 15, 2011).

Dale, Ronald J. "Battle of Crysler's Farm National Historic Site of Canada." *The Canadian Encyclopedia. www.thecanadianencyclopedia.com/index.cfm?PgNm=TCE&Params=A1ARTA0012346* (accessed November 1, 2011).

Dawe, Brian. "Thomas Ingersoll." Thomas Ingersoll of Oxford-on-the-Thames: Land Settlement by Township-granting in Upper Canada, 1792–1797. Introductory.pdf (application/ pdf. object) *home.connection.com/~wbdawe/Introductory.pdf* (accessed September 29, 2011).

Dictionary of Canadian Biography Online. "William Johnson Kerr." *biographi.ca/009004-119.01-e.php?&id_nbr=3477* (accessed September 7, 2011).

Files, Angela E.M. "Persecution of the Loyalists (Tories)." Fort Klock Historic Restoration. *threerivershms.com/loyalistspersecution.htm* (accessed October 3, 2011).

Henderson, Robert, ed. "An Account of the Battle of Ogdensburg, New York." The War of 1812 Website. *www.warof1812.ca/o_burg.htm* (accessed October 10, 2011).

Henderson, Robert. "The Capture of Fort George, May 27, 1813." The War of 1812 Website. *www.warof1812.ca/ftgeorge.htm* (accessed September 10, 2011).

Klinck, Carl F. "John Norton." *Dictionary of Canadian Biography Online. biographi.ca/009004-119.01-e.php?&id_nbr=3050* (accessed October 11, 2011).

McKenzie, Ruth. "James FitzGibbon." *Dictionary of Canadian Biography Online. biographi.ca/009004-119.01-e.php?id_nbr=4426* (accessed September 7, 2011).

Newfield, Gareth. "Blacks in Early Upper Canada." *The Canadian Encyclopedia. www.thecanadianencyclopedia.com/index.cfm?PgNm=TCE&Params=A1ARTA0012453* (accessed October 15, 2011).

Ontario Heritage Trust. "The Anti-Slavery Act of 1793." *www.heritagetrust.on.ca/Resources-and-Learning/Exhibits/John-Graves-Simcoe--Ontario-s-First-Lieutenant-Go/The-Anti-Slavery-Act-of-1793.aspx* (accessed November 15, 2011).

Parks Canada. "Fort Wellington National Historic Site of Canada." *www.pc.gc.ca/lhn-nhs/on/wellington/natcul.aspx* (accessed October 10, 2011).

Rawlyk, George A. "Richard Cartwright." *The Canadian Encyclopedia.* *www.thecanadianencyclopedia.com/index.cfm?PgNm=TCE&Params =A1ARTA0001445* (accessed October 15, 2011).

Talman, J.J. "William Hamilton Merritt." *Dictionary of Canadian Biography Online. biographi.ca/009004-119.01-e.php?&id_nbr=4597* (accessed October 11, 2011).

"Toronto Culture — Exploring Toronto's Past — A Provincial Centre, 1793–1851." City of Toronto, History Resources. *www.toronto.ca/culture/history/history-provincial-centre.htm* (accessed August 26, 2011).

"Welland Canal, Brief History." The Welland Canal Information Site. *www.wellandcanal.com/hist.htm* (accessed October 17, 2011).

Wilson, W.R. "Schools in Upper Canada." Early Canada Historical Narratives. *www.uppercanadahistory.ca/lteuc/lteuc6.html* (accessed October 3, 2011).

Index